The publisher gratefully acknowledges the
generous support of Edmund and Jeannie Kaufman
as members of the Literati Circle of the
University of California Press Foundation.

George Oppen

SELECTED PROSE, DAYBOOKS, AND PAPERS

George Oppen

Selected Prose, Daybooks, and Papers

EDITED BY STEPHEN COPE

University of California Press
Berkeley Los Angeles London

University of California Press
Berkeley and Los Angeles, California

University of California Press, Ltd.
London, England

Library of Congress Cataloging-in-Publication Data

Oppen, George.
Selected prose, daybooks, and papers / George Oppen ; edited by Stephen Cope.
p. cm.
Includes bibliographical references and index.
ISBN 978-0-520-23579-3 (cloth : alk. paper)—
ISBN 978-0-520-25232-5 (pbk. : alk. paper)
I. Cope, Stephen, 1972– II. Title.
PS3529.P54A6 2008
811'.5409—dc22 2007033593

Manufactured in Canada

16 15 14 13 12 11 10 09 08 07
10 9 8 7 6 5 4 3 2 1

The paper used in this publication is 50lb Rolland Enviro, 100% PCW natural sheet. It meets the minimum requirements of ANSI/NISO Z39.48–1992 (R 1997) (*Permanence of Paper*).

Contents

Acknowledgments

Portions of this manuscript in various stages of completion, and equipped with various editorial apparatuses, were published as follows: "A Selection from 'Daybook One,' 'Daybook Two,' and 'Daybook Three,' from *The Working Papers of George Oppen,*" *The Germ* 3 (Spring 1999): 192–253; "George Oppen: Twenty-six Fragments," *Facture* 2 (May 2001): 5–12 (reprinted in *The Best American Poetry 2002,* ed. Robert Creeley, series ed. David Lehman [New York. Scribner Poetry, 2002], 130–35; and in *George Oppen: Selected Poems,* ed. Robert Creeley [New York: New Directions, 2003], 183–90); "George Oppen: From 'Daybook Two,'" *Jubilat* 4 (2002): 40–55.

Additionally, other editors have produced the following selections from Oppen's archive, parts of which overlap with the present selection: "An Adequate Vision: A George Oppen Daybook," ed. Michael Davidson (*Ironwood* 26 [1985]: 5–35); "Meaning Is to Be Here: A Selection from the Daybook," ed. Cynthia Anderson (*Conjunctions* 10 [1987]: 186–208); "Selections from George Oppen's Daybook," ed. Dennis Young (*Iowa Review* 18, no. 3 [Fall 1988]: 1–17); and "The Circumstances," "Anthropologist of Myself," and "Philosophy of the Astonished," ed. Rachel Blau DuPlessis (*Sulfur* 25 [Fall 1989]: 10–43; 26 [Spring 1990]: 135–64; 27 [Fall 1990]: 202–20).

This project was aided by gracious funding from the Dorothy and Kenneth Hill Fellowship for Archival Research and a Dissertation Fellowship from the Literature Department at the University of California, San Diego. I also received invaluable assistance from two research fellowships, as well as a travel grant, from the Archive for New Poetry at Mandeville Special Collections Library at UCSD, where, without the help of Lynda Classen and, earlier, Bradley Westbrook (who first processed Oppen's archive when it arrived at the library), this project would have never gotten off the ground. Michael Davidson has seen this book through from its inception. Davidson's critical commentary on and intellectual support for this project have always been unwavering, and readers of the present book should applaud his dedication to Oppen scholarship. David Antin, Fanny Howe, Kathryn Shevelow, Donald Wesling, and William Arctander O'Brien each had valuable comments on a longer version of the manuscript that I submitted as a doctoral dissertation at the University of California, San Diego. Also at UCSD, Rae Armantrout, Melvyn Freilicher, John Granger, Douglas McCannell, Jerome and Diane Rothenberg, and Harleen Singh offered variously invaluable forms of support. David and Mary Jane Cope, my parents, offered encouragement and financial support during some lean years between academic appointments.

Needless to say, a project of this sort does not exist without the participation of a large community of scholars and readers. I will say it anyway. In addition to those mentioned above, each of the following has at some point offered commentary on the manuscript or assistance in tracking down or adding a citation, reference, or footnote: Rachel Blau DuPlessis, Gerald Bruns, Mika Court, Robert Creeley, Kevin Davies, Steve Dickinson, Steve Evans, Ben Friedlander, Christopher Funkhouser, Forrest Gander, Peter Gizzi, Lisa Jarnot, Daniel Kane, Kevin Killian, Joel Kuzsai, Hank Lazer, Andrew Maxwell, Linda Oppen, Michael Palmer, Marjorie Perloff, Dina Smith, Catherine Taylor, and Mark Weiss. Rachel Blau DuPlessis and Steve Dickinson deserve added praise for their remarkably generous, yet no less detailed and critical, attention to this manuscript in their capacity as "anonymous" readers for University of California Press. Three more properly anonymous readers were equally liberal with both their support and critique. Mary Severance and Andrew Frisardi, my project editor and copy editor, respectively, at UC Press, saved me much embarrassment in their careful review of the final manuscript. I consider Laura Cerutti, also at UC Press, to be a model editor.

Dickinson, via Kevin Killian, was kind enough to offer me the opportunity to present a commentary on these pages as "The George Oppen Memorial Lecture" in San Francisco in 1999, a series of lectures in which I remain honored to have participated.

In the final stages of this project, I found myself in Ithaca, New York, where Rachel Harms kindly offered me use of her laptop computer, a gesture that allowed the project to go forward. Neil and Marie Taylor were ideal hosts, who not only tolerated my presence in their house, but voluntarily shuttled me to and from Cornell University's library when my lack of a car made it impossible for me to get there otherwise. Catherine Taylor's tolerance, encouragement, and prodding made it possible for me to make deadlines that I otherwise would have missed.

Finally, additional thanks to Linda Oppen for her ongoing support, as well her gracious permission to reprint these writings. What is mine in this volume to dedicate, I dedicate to her.

Introduction

Forty-one years after the appearance of George Oppen's first book, *Discrete Series,* Hugh Kenner wrote of the publication of Oppen's *Collected Poems:* "All those years, academe (alas) is about to discover, an Oeuvre has been growing."[1] Were it possible for an oeuvre to grow posthumously, something similar might be said about what happened in the lengthy interval between Oppen's *Collected Poems* and his *Selected Prose, Daybooks, and Papers.* References to the Daybooks have peppered discussions of Oppen's work since the 1980s, as have quotations from both his Daybooks and Papers, drawn primarily from brief selections that have appeared in periodicals during that time. Quotations from "The Mind's Own Place" and "Three Poets"—often misidentified as his only two surviving works of commentary—have likewise abounded in critical writings devoted to Oppen. A transcription of Oppen's "Twenty-six Fragments" appeared in the 2002 edition of *The Best New American Poetry,* edited by Robert Creeley, as if to suggest that not only is Oppen's writing "news that stays news," to use Ezra Pound's famous phrase, but it is also *new* news, evidence of a literary oeuvre that is, for all practical purposes, still growing.[2]

Following on the heels of a new and expanded edition of Oppen's *Collected Poems* (edited by Michael Davidson), as well as a new *Selected Poems* (chosen by Robert Creeley), the present contribution to Oppen's available writings will no doubt help to sustain the recent surge of interest in his work.[3] Not that this interest ever waned for those aware of Oppen's lasting significance to modern and postmodern American poetry. He has long been regarded by those who read him as a—if not *the*—consummate model of poetic and ethical integrity. Emerging as a mature poet in the bohemian 1950s and 1960s, his intellectual sobriety and enduring desire to establish a language "of clarity, and of respect," as he put it in one poem, were considered by many to be as refreshing as they were noticeably out of step with prevailing fashion.[4] His interests were not in Eastern mysticism or the "crazy wisdom" of the Beats, nor in the subjective introspections of confessionalist verse. He was certainly no careerist in the academic sense, having put poetry aside for nearly twenty-five years to dedicate himself to what he considered more pressing social, political, and familial affairs. Even when he was awarded the Pulitzer Prize for poetry in 1969, Oppen was ambivalent: "It is, in view of the record," he wrote to poet and *New York Times Book Review* editor Harvey Shapiro, "a questionable compliment" (*SL* 195). Poetry for Oppen, rather than being about fame or even public recognition, was a "test of truth," a "determination to find the image, the thing encountered, the thing seen each day whose meaning has become the meaning and the color of our lives."[5] He conceived of it as an arduous task, insisting that each poem—in fact, that each word in each poem—be painstakingly earned.

Little wonder, then, that his published oeuvre would seem so modest when compared with those of his predecessors and contemporaries. He wrote no poem of epic scale such as Ezra Pound's *Cantos,* William Carlos Williams's *Paterson,* or Louis Zukofsky's *A;* his books were notoriously slim volumes containing slight, wrought lyrics and minutely crafted serial poems. His self-prepared *Collected Poems* (1975) was smaller in size than many a fellow poet's *Selected.* Even smaller was his output of prose. At a time when essays, manifestos, and critical reviews seemed part and parcel of a poet's vocation, Oppen's justifications and defenses of his poetics remained for the most part private, circulated in letters to a close coterie of poets, friends, and relatives.[6] In contrast to Pound, Williams, Zukofsky, T. S. Eliot, Gertrude Stein, and, later, Charles Olson, Robert Creeley, Adrienne Rich, and Amiri Baraka / LeRoi Jones (to name but a few), Oppen's published prose consisted of a single essay in poetics, a handful of interviews, and the several short reviews and notes gathered here. Also, unlike many twentieth-century poets, he never tried his hand at fiction or drama, for his work resisted dramatic narrative arcs as much as it refused traditional modes of exposition and argumentation. He sought discrete moments of clarity, sincerity, epiphany, and vision—"lyric valuables" (*NCP* 50; *SP* 15)—whose scarcity required what he called in a late poem "the rare poetic / Of veracity" (*NCP* 215; *SP* 124), an art of precision and detail involving minute rather than grandiose attentions.

The present volume demonstrates, however, that despite his public reticence, Oppen's attention to poetics was assiduous. "I work sometimes for eight hours or so, fiddling with corrections," he writes in Daybook II: II: "But sometimes I am so tired in two or three hours of effort that I'm shaken. Possible [*sic*] an element of self dramatization. But it is also fear. I ~~realize that~~ nothing so extraordinary appears in the poems . . ." (see p. 78). And, indeed, it does not: the corrections, overwrites, and general unsettledness of Oppen's Daybook writings are unique to the singular medium that Oppen reserved for poetics, precisely because this poetics was one that involved not abstractions but the immediate "nightmare of bric-a-brac" (Daybook I; p. 56) that he everywhere refuses to resolve into comforting wholes. "It would not be terrifying in abstract terms," he concludes the passage above: "It is terrifying in terms of the objects around me" (Daybook II:II; p. 78). Oppen's poetics is always just so embedded in the phenomenal world. He deals with specificities that complicate generalities as opposed to confirming them.

Oppen arrived at such a poetics early. He was a charter member of the "Objectivist" school that also included Zukofsky, Charles Reznikoff, Carl Rakosi, Basil Bunting, and Lorine Niedecker. Each in varying ways extended the practice of spare and exacting verse that earlier modernist writers like Williams, Pound, and H.D. had sought as a remedy to what they perceived as the heightened rhetorical platitudes of nineteenth-century writing.[7] Yet "Objectivism" differed from this earlier Modernism in its often leftist political leanings, as well as its primarily urban, Jewish and working class roots.[8] More than one critic has argued that Oppen, and Objectivism as a whole, are closer in sensibility to postmodernist tendencies like Language Poetry than to the more politically (if not aesthetically) conservative modernists like Eliot and Pound.[9] Oppen especially sought to challenge Imagism on the grounds that it retained a kind of gentility that was foreign to the exigencies of modern life: "it was not an unimportant stance," he writes of Zukofsky's defining introduction to *The Objectivists Anthology* (1932), "against the liquidation of poetry into the sentimentalism of the American so-called Imagists" (*SL* 139). Later he would insist upon "[t]he image as a test of sincerity, as against . . . a 'picture' intended for the delectation of the reader who may be imagined to admire the quaintness and ingenuity of the poet, but can scarcely have been part of the poet's attempt to find himself in the world—unless perhaps to find himself as a charming conversationalist" (*SL* 146). In Daybook II Oppen is equally disparaging: "The weakness of Imagism—a man writes of the moon rising over a pier who knows nothing about piers and is disregarding all that he knows about the moon" (Daybook II:III; p. 82). For Oppen—who was employed at various times as a carpenter, construction worker, and factory worker—the issue of "craft" in poetry was more than merely metaphorical, and the Objectivist emphasis on "the necessity of form, the objectification of the poem" (*SL* 139), was thus felt by him, as by the other Objectivists, as a matter of honesty rather than posture.

Zukofsky defined the quintessential Objectivist attitude as "sincerity," an aesthetic in which "writing occurs which is the detail, not mirage, of seeing, of thinking with things as they exist."[10] Robert Creeley repeats this definition in discussing Oppen's "complex 'thinking with his poems'" as "a consistent and major factor in all his surviving work" (*SP* xi). With the exception of Zukofsky, the Objectivists did indeed focus their aesthetic and ethical practice almost exclusively on their poetry, rather than in secondary writings.[11] Because of this, their status as a well-defined group with a well-defined set of aesthetic principles and goals is provisional at best. Even Zukofsky refused to consider himself either the founder or the champion of a new poetic doctrine, and he was often at pains to insist that the Objectivist appellation coined by him in a 1931 issue of *Poetry* that featured the aforementioned group (sans Niedecker, plus a few others) ought not to have suggested that they were a unified front along the lines of other literary movements or schools. For his part, Oppen agreed: "Undoubtedly the Objectivists differed from each other," he wrote in 1974 letter to Martin Rosenblum, who had reviewed his book *Seascape: Needle's Eye*. "And drastically. I believe I thought of these poets simply as the poets I found revelatory. I have no memory at all of having felt myself to be arguing or supporting a theoretical (technical) position" (*SL* 284). Such a refusal of canon is characteristic of Oppen. Edward Hirsch, in a 2003 *Washington Post* column on Oppen's work, went so far as to question Oppen's group affiliation outright: "Oppen . . . is widely known as an Objectivist poet, but I think of him more as an American solitary, akin to Edward Hopper."[12] Although the wording here is questionable—

"iconoclast" might have been a bit better, given Oppen's prominent role as a longtime labor organizer and political activist (hardly "solitary" activities)—that Oppen went against the grain in both his life and his work is indisputable.

This singularity is everywhere apparent in Oppen's *Selected Prose, Daybooks, and Papers.* Although Oppen's letters—with their customarily idiosyncratic and discontinuous use of typography, spacing, punctuation, and the like—display a unique care with respect to the usually extemporaneous epistolary mode, the *Selected Prose, Daybooks, and Papers* contains work that is patently different, in form and often theme, from that which usually constitutes a poet's supplemental body of prose. There are no manifestos here, no poetic platforms, few histrionic proclamations, no clearly stated affinity with this or that literary movement. He pledges few allegiances to any strictly theorized poetics, preferring instead to encounter, discuss, and evaluate his own and others' writings on their own terms. His thought is rarely prescriptive; it is always first and foremost *explorative* in the sense that he conceived the term, by means of an analogy, in a mid-1960s Daybook entry:

> A man, finding himself in possession of a number of opinions which he would like to express, writes an essay
>
> an explorer or a mathematician also knows what he thinks—but doesn't know what he will find   a man applying a method of thought as which is powerful in itself, which is more powerful than the ordinary forms of discourse, doesn't know what he will find, or what he will think (Daybook II:V; p. 121)

An "explorer or mathematician," not an expositor or theoretician: this is how Oppen conceived of himself as a writer. Consequently, his writings behave more like findings or discoveries than they do like aesthetic inventions, self-expressions, or opinions.

This is especially so in Oppen's Daybooks and Papers, the writings which constitute the greater part of the present volume. For it is in these writings that Oppen—like the proverbial good mathematician—most palpably "shows his work." But it is also true to a large extent of Oppen's prose. "The Mind's Own Place," the closest Oppen came to producing a poetic platform, was roundly criticized by its initial readers for lacking a clearly articulated poetics.[13] His self-titled "Statement on Poetics" is less that than a brief and occasional meditation on prosody. Short pieces such as "A Letter" and "Nonresistance" are visibly truncated, fragmentary, hypothetical, provisional (note the preponderance of "ifs" in the latter). They display what Rachel Blau DuPlessis, discussing Oppen's poetry, calls "the inner dynamic of gnomic fragments," as they all but abandon gestures towards unequivocal closure (*MP* 146). Even "The Mind's Own Place" concludes with a question mark.

In this sense, one might regard Oppen's *Selected Prose, Daybooks, and Papers* as writings spawned from the kind of "negative capability" that instigates his composition of poetry. "The poet learns almost everything from his own verse," he says in the aforementioned "Statement." Similarly, in a letter to Robert Duncan: "We do not know before we complete the poem. Neither of us write[s] what we already know, and of course that's the essential life of the poem" (*SL* 270). Although perhaps not a noteworthy sentiment for a poet—John Keats, after all, first defined "negative capability" as "when a man is capable of being in uncertainties, mysteries, doubts, without any irritable reaching after fact and reason"—applied to the writings gathered here, the practice amounts to a unique disturbance of generic norms and formal protocols.[14] Aphoristic and apothegmatic, and yet also curiously open-ended and incomplete, Oppen's "prose" constitutes a unique intermingling of reflection, critique, and assertion that acquires and achieves its idiosyncratic form not by accident but by necessity.

But it is not only this brand of "negative capability" that generates Oppen's thinking. What I have taken to calling to his "negative culpability" is equally pervasive in his work, for as much as any other twentieth-century poet, Oppen held himself and his verse accountable to stringent ethical as well as aesthetic demands. His life certainly provided no shortage of opportunities for him to weigh his own responsibilities (if not liabilities).[15] Born on April 24, 1908, in New Rochelle, New York, into a fully assimilated, upper-class Jewish family (his father, George August Oppenheimer, was the son of a diamond merchant who in 1927 shortened the family name to Oppen), Oppen's mother, Elsie Rothfeld, fatally shot herself in 1912 after a series of nervous breakdowns. Oppen's older sister, Elizabeth (Libby), seven at the time of their mother's death, would die in 1960, in what the coroner ruled a suicide. These deaths took place within the context of a familial wealth and privilege with which Oppen would remain perennially uncomfortable. As he writes dismissively (yet conflictedly) to Philip Levine in 1970, apropos a brief "autobiography":

> —born of a couple of rather millionaire lines—in the generation of my father, aunts, uncles becoming something on the order of the International Set, etc . . . Disastrous, of course. My mother's suicide when I was four, an elder sister's suicide, my mother's sister———among the males———commitments, deaths———[. . .]
> a childhood of nurses, butlers and what not—(it's why I know how to sail)—and minor inheritances along the way [. . .] and finally a "big" that is, a big enough inheritance, tho I have no older relatives who would have found it so (*SL* 207–8)

"I don't know if [my] books could have been written if I had worked to the age of retirement," Oppen continues. "I think they would not have, and I think [. . .] that is a terrible thing to say. We had help from the dead. Who wanted to die" (*SL* 208).

Oppen would experience similar deaths in close proximity. After his father remarried and the family moved to San Francisco, Oppen was expelled from military school in 1925 for his role as the driver in a fatal, alcohol-related car accident. "Imagine a man in the ditch," he would later write in "Route," alluding to the experience:

> The wheels of the overturned wreck
> Still spinning—
>
> I don't mean he despairs, I mean if he does not
> He sees in the manner of poetry (*NCP* 198)

He would later (April 22, 1945) be the sole survivor of a company of three soldiers who were pinned in a foxhole in Alsace by direct gunfire during the Battle of the Bulge. Oppen's wounds earned him a Purple Heart, among other medals. His war experience underwrites, directly or indirectly, a number of his later poems, including, most notably, "Of Being Numerous" and "Route." But Oppen never played the hero. In section 14 of "Of Being Numerous," for instance:

> I cannot even now
> Altogether disengage myself
> From those men
>
> With whom I stood in emplacements, in mess tents,
> In hospitals and sheds and hid in the gullies
> Of blasted roads in a ruined country,
>
> Among them many men
> More capable than I—
>
> Muykut and a sergeant
> Named Healy,
> That lieutenant also—
>
> How forget that? How talk
> Distantly of "The People" (*NCP* 171; *SP* 91)

And later (section 20): "I know // Failure and the guilt / Of failure" (*NCP* 174; *SP* 95). Oppen's attempt in "Non-Resistance, etc. Or: Of the Guiltless" to explain or justify—or even to simply come to terms with—his war experience is an especially conflicted one, achieving more of a resonant impasse than any comforting conclusion. That it is presented as a series of conditional hypotheses only serves to reinforce the inscrutability of the conflict, even its ineffability: "If I killed, I would suffer guilt. If I did not, I would suffer . . . I don't even know a word, a name for what I would suffer" (p. 46).

Oppen's sense of "culpability," however, was not strictly a matter of guilt. To the contrary, his reputation as a literary and ethical model has very much to do with his sense of responsibility and the variously anachronistic decisions that it would inspire him to make throughout his life and career. His uneasiness with respect to his childhood of "nurses, butlers and what not" was reflected early on in his rebellious adolescence and, after having belatedly obtained a high school degree in 1926, in his almost whimsical decision to leave San Francisco for Oregon, where a friend was to attend college. It was there that he met lifelong companion Mary Colby (later Mary Oppen), and there that he was first introduced to Conrad Aiken's anthology *Modern American Poetry*. Both meetings were seminal. In Mary Oppen's words, they were exhilarated to find that "poetry was being written in our times" (*ML* 61). The two left college shortly thereafter when Mary was expelled and George severely punished for violating curfew. The violation was both romantic and rebellious, and Oppen later memorialized the evening in "The Forms of Love."

> Parked in the fields
> All night
> So many years ago,
> We saw
> A lake beside us
> When the moon rose.
> I remember
>
> Leaving that ancient car
> Together. I remember
> Standing in the white grass
> Beside it. We groped
> Our way together
> Downhill in the bright
> Incredible light
>
> Beginning to wonder
> Whether it could be lake
> Or fog
> We saw, our heads
> Ringing under the stars we walked
> To where it would have wet our feet
> Had it been water (*NCP* 106)

The feelings of wonderment, exploration, and discovery that animate the poem would remain with the couple for years, if not a lifetime. The subjunctive note on which the poem concludes ("would have"/"had it been") would also remain as a staple of Oppen's poetry, evidence of an uneasiness with respect to positivism and the assumptions upon which any undue confidence might rest.

The Oppens felt a similar unease with respect to the comforts of inherited family and home, and after their expulsion, their life was largely itinerant. They hitchhiked across the country, marrying in 1927 in Texas using pseudonyms (George was "David Verdi"). They returned briefly to San Francisco, but conflicts between Oppen and his family sent them back on the road. Hitchhiking again, they arrived in Detroit in 1928, where they purchased a boat and sailed by way of the Great Lakes to Brooklyn—the first of many trips by boat the two would take together throughout their lives. In Brooklyn, Oppen first encountered Zukofsky's poetry, and later met him, Reznikoff, and Williams. In 1929, the couple relocated to France, using part of a substantial inheritance released to Oppen on his twenty-first birthday to found To Publishers (with Zukofsky as editor), which printed Williams's *A Novelette and Other Prose (1921–1931),* Pound's *How to Read,* and Zukofsky's own *An "Objectivists" Anthology.* A planned edition of the complete prose of Ezra Pound never appeared. The Oppens returned to the United States in 1933, having dissolved To Publishers and initiated (again, with Zukofsky) the Objectivist Press, which published self-financed books by Reznikoff and Williams, as well as, in 1934, Oppen's first book, *Discrete Series.*

For twenty-five years, this was known as Oppen's only contribution to the literary world. In 1935, disillusioned by unemployment and poverty, and galvanized by the Popular Front, the Oppens joined the Communist Party and Oppen's writing ceased. Again, Oppen's iconoclasm and his sense of culpability merged. As he conceived it, his decision to stop writing involved a separation between the poetic and the political, the ethical and the literary. In an interview with Tom Mandel and Burton Hatlen, for instance: "It's a narrow public for poetry. It always will be. We didn't dream of addressing the crowds with poetry. And we distinguished, as I said, between poetry and politics" (*MP* 33). In letters and interviews, Oppen often repeated approvingly Hugh Kenner's famous remark that his silence essentially meant that it took him "25 years to write the next poem," a summation that Mandel, writing to Hatlen in a letter later appended to the published version of their interview, derides on social and political grounds:

> I hoped [Oppen] would out with having written just not published during those years; just because it seems a questionable move when someone abandons the art as not holding enough for him, "not the most important thing in the world" [Oppen's phrase, from the interview], as if, *a seeker,* one would go only to that "most important thing." But wouldn't that be just the poet's task, to make it important? It may easily seem to another poet that not much good poetry would get written on the basis of such impulses as this of George's. Nor does Kenner's "in short it took 25 years to write the next poem" help it all, since that's not what happened but rather a metaphor enabling one to look away from what happened. (*MP* 49)

Mandel's complaint is commonplace among Oppen's readers, especially insofar as Kenner's quip is concerned. For Oppen, however, it was not that "art [did not hold] enough for him," but rather that that Socialist proscriptions on art would have limited his poetry's vision to an unacceptable extent. In this, his position did not waver. Writing in Daybook II of John Howard Lawson, founder of the Screen Writers' Guild, and his cohort: they "are fine enough people, but they are people who long ago somehow acquired the vocation of arguing with artists. They happen to be color-blind, tone deaf" (Daybook II:I; p. 70). And elsewhere: "art and political action are in precise opposition in this regard: that it can always be quite easily shown that political action is going to be valuable; it is difficult to ever prove [that it has been]. . . . Whereas art is precisely the opposite case" (Daybook II:III; p. 89). The Depression, the rise of fascism, and the prevalence of urban poverty made the short-term goals of "political action" much more crucial for Oppen than the long-term aims of art. And as Eliot Weinberger points out, Oppen refused to write "stirring doggerel or prose propaganda" (*NCP* vii).

Thus, despite Mandel's "hope," Oppen was not writing during his hiatus. The Oppens instead dedicated themselves wholeheartedly to political work, organizing strikes in Utica, New York, and Kings County, in the latter of which Oppen served as campaign manager for the Communist Party elections in 1936. After working as a pattern maker for an aircraft company, in 1942 Oppen moved to Detroit in order to be inducted into the Army; his antifascist sentiments required of him, he thought, that he participate in the efforts against Hitler. The decision inspired the remarkable meditations in "Nonresistance, etc.; or, Of the

Guiltless," and his time at war would haunt him as well as his poetry throughout his life.

Upon returning from the war (injured), George settled with Mary and their daughter, Linda (b. 1940), in Southern California, where George purchased a small piece of property and constructed the family's home. They remained active in leftist politics, but were increasingly distancing themselves from Party politics. During this time, the FBI opened what would amount to an extensive file on the Oppens, visiting the family several times and keeping close tabs on their activities. Such harassment led them, after much forethought, to relocate to Mexico, where they fell in with an extensive group of blacklisted screenwriters and artists, including Julian Zimet and Charles Humboldt (with whom Oppen would keep in touch for many years after), the composer Conlon Nancarrow, screenwriters Hugo Butler, Ian Hunter, Ring Lardner, Jr., and others.[16] Oppen worked at odd jobs in Mexico, and from 1951 to 1955, attended the art school Escuela de Pintura y Escultura Esmeralda, where he learned wood carving. He used the GI Bill to finance the education.

Little is known of the Oppens' time in Mexico; the couple—especially George—were notoriously tight-lipped, and with the exception of a few scattered phrases here and there, the FBI files are of little help (much has been blackened out). In 1958, George had his famous "rust in copper" dream, recounted by Mary Oppen in her autobiography:

> (George) and his sister were going through his father's papers after his father's death. In a file marked "miscellaneous" was a paper entitled "How to Prevent Rust in Copper." George thought, "My old man was a little frivolous perhaps, but he certainly knew that copper does not rust." He shook the bed with his laughter . . . (*ML* 202)

In 1965, Oppen wrote to John Crawford of the dream: "I reacted . . . with elation, in fact hilarity. I was driving somewhere the following morning, and found myself swerving the car from one side of the road to the other—deliberately—and howling with laughter. . . . I was laughing at a small thing in the dream, and one which was not really very funny. An excuse for elation, a false excuse for a real elation" (*SL* 127). Oppen was driving to visit Mary's psychiatrist, who informed him that he was "dreaming that (he didn't) want to rust" (*ML* 202), and, humorously, that "copper" was code for "Oppen." The dream led Oppen, for reasons that are not clear, to begin writing again. His first new poem (1958) was "Blood from a Stone" (*NCP* 52–54; *SP* 16–18).

Thus resumed Oppen's career as a poet. The couple returned permanently to the United States in 1960, eventually settling in San Francisco. *The Materials* was published in 1962 by New Directions with help from the *San Francisco Review,* where George's half-sister and lifelong confidant June Oppen Degnan was editor. *This in Which* followed shortly thereafter, in 1965. Oppen was awarded the Pulitzer Prize in Poetry in 1969 for the 1968 volume *Of Being Numerous* (New Directions), the title poem of which is an extended serial work that is the closest Oppen came to producing a "long poem." Oppen published two more original books—*Seascape: Needle's Eye* (Sumac Press, 1972) and *Primitive* (Black Sparrow Press, 1978)—as well as one notable chapbook, *Alpine* (Perishable Press, 1969).While assembling the 1975 edition of his *Collected Poems* for New Directions, Oppen added a last section of new poems that he titled *Myth of the Blaze (1972–1975). Primitive* was assembled with Mary's secretarial assistance, as Oppen was by the time of its publication developing symptoms of Alzheimer's disease. He would succumb to the disease on July 24, 1984, in Sunnyvale, California.

Because of Oppen's "negative culpability" and the complex intermingling of guilt, responsibility, and openness that the term implies, he is sometimes compared to poets like Paul Celan or Edmond Jabès, both Holocaust survivors whose responses to the war and its aftermath, as well as to the complexities and horrors of the twentieth century, are enigmatic and profound.[17] Yet even as he read widely in European philosophy—Hegel, Heidegger, Maritain, and Wittgenstein, served his thinking especially well—Oppen's grounding in American modernism cannot be denied. The Objectivist emphasis on form is certainly apparent everywhere in the lapidary structures of his most memorable poems. Oppen's life and thought, as reflected in his *Prose, Daybooks, and Papers,* demonstrate that for him, Objectivism never simply meant "objectivity," nor even that the world was itself an object. Rather, the world for Oppen remained an *objective*—something to be fought for and achieved through praxis rather than merely reflected or represented in his art.

•

EDITORIAL CONSIDERATIONS

The George Oppen archive, housed in the Archive for New Poetry at Mandeville Special Collections Library at the University of California, San Diego, consists of thousands of pages of Oppen's published and previously unpublished writings. These writings vary in kind from letters (completed letters and drafts, sent and unsent), drafts of poems (again, both completed and abandoned), reading notes, writing notes, and that which comprises the bulk of the collection: Oppen's Daybooks and a voluminous archive of poem drafts, drafts of letters, aphoristic reflections, and incidental writings gathered under the heading "Notes, Jottings, etc." *Selected Prose, Daybooks, and Papers* consists of an edition of Oppen's previously published prose, a selection from his five Daybooks, and "Twenty-six Fragments," scraps of paper and notes pasted to Oppen's wall or found on or near his desk after his death.

With the exception of "Statement on Poetics," all of the writings gathered here under the heading "Prose" were published during Oppen's lifetime. I have reproduced as faithfully as possible Oppen's often anomalous spacing and typography. The "Statement" was transcribed by Kathryn Shevelow shortly after Oppen's death, and I have used her transcription here. The notes are mine.

The Daybooks are small, makeshift books bound by Oppen using various ready-to-hand materials (pipe-stem cleaners, nails and wood, paste, glue). They were initially given their title by Michael Davidson, in one of the first selections from Oppen's archive to have been published.[18] I have retained the title for this volume for two reasons: (1) the term usefully distinguishes between bound and unbound materials, the latter of which I refer to, simply, as "Papers"; (2) the term has passed into general usage among readers of Oppen's work, and thus to adapt a new title now would likely generate more confusion than it would alleviate any minor inaccuracies that might attend such a label.

The Daybooks date primarily, but not exclusively, from the early 1960s (ca. 1962) until Oppen's completion of the book *Of Being Numerous* (1969), although notes in the margins and references to historical events that took place prior to 1960 suggest that some of these pages were composed prior to 1962, while references to later works suggest with equal certainty that Oppen revisited the writings gathered in his Daybooks after 1969. Daybook V, in particular, was most likely bound after Oppen had completed a draft of his fifth book, *Seascape: Needle's Eye* (1972), as the last pages consist of four variously epigraphed flyleaves for the book (then titled "Of the Needle's Eye"). In general, dating this material conclusively is impossible, as Oppen returned often to pages—in many instances, years later—to add to or revise his earlier thoughts, and he bound the material with little if any chronological consideration. I have conjectured about dates where possible and appropriate.

It is worth noting, however, that the lack of chronology—indeed, the lack of any overarching organizational principle here—might be considered as much an enabling characteristic of this work as one of its limitations. For the recurrence of thoughts, phrases, or verses in different contexts is characteristic of Oppen's writing. "A Language of New York," published in *This in Which* as a complete poem, is later revised and expanded to become "Of Being Numerous" in the book of the same title; while the limited-edition volume *Alpine* (1969) used phrases from *This in Which,* published half a decade earlier, before being radically revised and included in *Myth of the Blaze, 1972–1975* (1975). "The Forms of Love," a poem of Oppen's that, according to Mary Oppen's autobiography (*ML* 62), recounts their first night together in the mid-1920s, first appeared nearly four decades later, in 1964 (see the excerpt from this poem, above). To identify the sequence in which Oppen's poems have appeared in the various editions of his collected works as chronological in nature is thus in itself often erroneous. To attempt to do so with a set of documents such as these—where no authorial considerations of sequencing are evident—would be to impose a structure in which less would be gained in terms of biographical or chronological accuracy than would be lost in terms of textual vitality.

This is not to suggest, however, that the Daybooks exist in an ahistorical vacuum, or that their relationship to Oppen's published poetry is negligible. Even as the strictest biographical concerns of Oppen scholars may be frustrated by the lack of a familiar time line, Oppen's historical references are numerous, and I have identified these as much as possible in my notes. But since Oppen's practice of writing often involved the cutting up of phrases from one sheet of paper and then pasting them on to another, or of reproducing by hand, in various stages of revision, phrases, paragraphs, stanzas, and the like on numerous pages (again, often over a period of some years), ascribing a strict date to any single page, not to mention an entire Daybook, would offer at best a spurious principle of organization. Therefore, in introducing each section of each Daybook with a brief and at times conjectural historical contextualization, my aim has been to offer scholars potential avenues for further research, rather than to nail down any definitive sense of linear or historical progression in these writings.

Because of this, my editorial approach rests on the basic assumption that these pages represent—in both original and transcribed form—not merely the ready-made products of thought compressed into one or another genre, nor solely cultural or biographical artifacts offered up for consumption by cultural historians. Rather, they are traces of a process of thought and writing that operates independently of any narrow, formal concern. Akin in this sense to notebooks, journals, diaries, and the like, these papers are finally none of these; nor are they fully letters, essays, or aphoristic statements. They are an admixture and more, and thus they fall outside the purview of any institutional tendency toward formal or generic normalization. They comprise an *incomplete* work—a partial and diffuse commentary the nature of which requires that they remain so.

To present the material in an accurate manner is thus to preserve its incompleteness in both specific and general terms. As a given page or strain of thought remains partial and unresolved, so too the work as a whole resists finalities. In relation to this incompletion, Oppen's oeuvre as it appears in the various editions of his collected work might be read, not as a closed or final project that delimits the horizons of his work, but as a collection of poems that are themselves the modular structures in which his thought finds occasional rest. As Michael Davidson argues and I enthusiastically agree, the "ideal of a poetry that no longer represents but participates in the process of thought" is not often considered with respect to Oppen: "It is as though we have focused only on the first word in the title to his first book, *Discrete Series,* to the exclusion of the second."[19] Both poems and working papers arise from and through such participation—a practice of which the published work is not the polished performance but the temporary (and tenuous) manifestation, a kind of rehearsal, say, of which the writing is the material evidence and not the grand finale.

Therefore, my goal as compiler, transcriber, and editor has been not just to present a selection from Oppen's Daybooks, but to preserve as accurately as possible their anomalous and idiosyncratic form. Nevertheless, as with any editorial endeavor, some measure of *practical* editorial intervention has been necessary in approaching this material. By "practical" I mean to denote: (1) The volume of unpublished materials housed in the archive would render a complete presentation of every leaf contained in a given Daybook not only burdensome but, due to the preponderance of early drafts of currently published poems and letters (new and/or properly critical editions of which would prove inconsequentially distinct from the already existent editions), relatively uninteresting to any but the most serious scholar of Oppen's process of revision. Such scholars have and will continue to use the archive itself as a resource for their investigations. (2) The illegibility of the material—particularly of Oppen's handwriting—has occasioned the intervention of a textual apparatus developed to clarify, formally but not semantically, those passages which would be otherwise indecipherable.

In the first case, the material presented here is restricted to a selection from those documents that cannot be considered working drafts of published poems or published letters. This is to make the distinction between papers and drafts, the former of which, although often containing the seeds of poems, and sometimes containing full stanzas of published poems alongside other unpublished material (with Oppen's editorial commentary or not), have in most cases been preserved, while the latter—often up to a dozen leaves with minimal variation—have been excised. I have also excised purely ephemeral writings (shopping lists, phone numbers, addresses, and the like), as well as altogether illegible writings. Decisions regarding inclusion and exclusion have been made as often as possible at the level of the page rather than that of the phrase or fragment. This is a decision meant to preserve Oppen's practice of using the page as a unit of composition, as well as to preserve the enigmatic and anomalous juxtapositions (intentional or not) that often appear on a given page. Some extreme cases have required more extensive editorial intervention on my part. The page represented in figure 2 (Daybook II: I), for example, is the first of several typescript drafts that Oppen extensively edited, the last of which I used as the basis of my transcription. However, I felt it important to include the holograph note dated "1969" that appears at the bottom of the first draft, not only because it appears likely that this was Oppen's last addition to any of the drafts, but also in order to document Oppen's practice of returning to and revising these papers over an extended period of time. Thus, in this case, as in a few others, my transcriptions are based on several drafts of a single passage from which I've compiled a representation that is equally faithful to Oppen's thoughts and revision. In all cases, my decisions regarding inclusion or exclusion are meant to demonstrate both the character and range of Oppen's writing without sacrificing either legibility or general accessibility. Finally, it is worth emphasizing here that this selection is precisely that: a selection from Oppen's archive, and not necessarily a replacement for active scholarly research.

In the second case, a method of transcription has been developed, the primary precedent for which is the notion of "plain text" as formulated by Edgar Marquess Branch, Michael B. Frank, and Kenneth M. Sanderson in the introduction to *Mark Twain's Letters,* volume 1 (1853–66): "The letters have been transcribed using a system of notation and a rationale for emendation which have not before been used to edit letters. We call the result 'plain text,' in contrast both to 'clear text' and its opposite, 'genetic text.' We require two things of every transcription in plain text: (a) it must be sufficiently faithful to the text of the letter to serve as a *reliable substitute* for it; and (b) it must be *easier to read than the original letter,* so long as its reliability is preserved intact." In the case of Oppen's writings, the editorial interventions required by plain-text transcription primarily have to do with handwriting, margin justification, insertion of text, and occasionally spelling. The justifications and editorial markers pertinent to the application of plain text are enumerated in the "Textual Apparatus" note in the front matter of this volume.

Textual Apparatus

1. Unless otherwise noted, all marks and inscriptions—such as parentheses ( ), ellipses (. . .), crossed-out passages *(~~strikethrough~~)*, bullets (•), etc.—are transpositions of Oppen's own. Brackets [ ] indicate editorial text (see number 6, below).
2. New pages are distinguished by the symbol +++.
3. Regular font face *(*regular*)* is used for passages typed by Oppen.
4. Italicized print (*italics*) denotes handwritten inscriptions in the genetic text.
5. Insertion Arrows ^ and ^ denote the beginning and end of text inserted in the genetic text by arrows, lines, or inscriptions within margins and between lines. This serves both to preserve Oppen's intentions with regards to revision and to render the document more legible. (When marginal inscription indicates the deletion of a word and its replacement by another, the deleted word is rendered in ~~strikethrough~~ with the inserted word adjacent to the deleted word.)
6. Brackets ([ ]) denote text that is altogether illegible. This is predominantly handwritten text; in some instances, conjectures have been made regarding potential readings—for example, [*force? farce?*].
7. Spacing has been reproduced as accurately as possible, with the exception of passages that were clearly typed as prose, and in which line ends generate no significant meaning. Such passages have been normalized and wrapped accordingly.
8. Following the precedent established by Rachel Blau DuPlessis in her edition of Oppen's letters, spelling has been normalized except where an anomaly generates meanings germane to the context of Oppen's poetics. (Due to the preponderance of typographical errors, this is a practical consideration.)

9. Also following DuPlessis, capitalization has been normalized only where it appears to be an unintentional typographical glitch, such as the second letter of a capitalized word by which potential or alternative meanings and connotations do not appear plausible. Oppen's idiosyncratic capitalization of first-person singular pronouns, proper nouns, and the opening words of sentences have been retained where these instances occur in the genetic text.
10. For Daybook V I have added a thick rule to signal text pasted by Oppen over other text or onto a given page. See introduction to Daybook V.

Prose

Three Poets

Published in *Poetry* 100, no. 5 (August 1962): 329–33. A review of Allen Ginsberg, *Kaddish and Other Poems, 1958–1960* (San Francisco: City Lights, 1961); Charles Olson, *Maximus from Dogtown* (San Francisco: Auerhahn Press, 1961), and *The Distances* (New York: Grove Press, 1961); and Michael McClure, *Dark Brown* (San Francisco: Auerhahn Press, 1961). The limited editions of *Dark Brown* and *Maximus from Dogtown* that Oppen reviewed are both unpaginated; in the notes, I have supplied page numbers of more recent editions. The Auerhahn Press edition of *Maximus from Dogtown* includes a brief introduction by McClure.

+ + +

In the lines of Ginsberg's *Kaddish* is evoked the passionate and destroyed body of a woman who pursues a world which is not hers and which does not become hers.[1] In the poet's prayer for the dead is the sound of the man wrenched from the past by horror and compassion: in that isolation and clarity is the terror of myth and its sense of the ultimate threats. It is not a poem which could be easily forgotten. Everywhere reflecting Whitman and Lindsay and the width of the American past, the poem moves its final sections through the heavy bars of the traditional Hebrew prayer. It is a poem of very great power, of very great "mass." It is also a poem of visual acuity, and often of startling verbal precision, avoiding nothing in its path. It is not, to say again, a poem which could easily be forgotten.

The fifteen shorter poems of the book are of uneven quality. Ginsberg, of course, means to embrace that risk. It would be pointless to object to the expanded form of the poems since copiousness is an essential part not only of Ginsberg's gift but of his program. This is declamatory form: to quarrel with that is simply to quarrel with the heart of his work. In *Kaddish* this expansiveness produces, at least, a great and rare virtue: the poem cannot be misunderstood. It can be read at the tempo of speech. But the danger for Ginsberg in the shorter pieces is that there may be nowhere for him to go if he is to rely on declamation, that he might be stuck on too high and too declamatory a note. There need be nothing ephemeral about the lyric poet who responds passionately and in his own way to his vision, but if the poet begins to ask us to accept a system of opinions and attitudes he must manage the task of rigorous thought. There is behind some of these poems an argument, an opinion, even an exhortation which not only invites reply but sometimes impatient reply, and in many others an air of having attempted to force a poem, of having hoped for a poem by riding "no hands." It may be that Ginsberg's sense of his audience is too immediate, and it may be the wrong audience. Ginsberg must be aware of this danger: it is a question of the line between histrionics and openness, the lack of preciousness which is at least a part of the value of this work and its impact. It may be that these poems are necessary preparation for work as firm and significant as *Kaddish*.

Maximus from Dogtown is obviously not part of Olson's best work. The book is a single poem based on the anecdote of a man killed while attempting to wrestle a bull. Some of the verse appears to be creating unnecessary difficulties for itself, as if lacking sufficient motivation:

> . . . trying
> to get the young bull down
> to see if Sunday morning again he might
> before the people show off . . .[2]

I do not know a reason for this, nor does there seem to be a reason to construct again—in eight pages of verse—the metaphor of the earth as woman and death as the male act. The poem ends:

> Then only
> . . .
> did the earth
> let her robe
> uncover and her part
> take him in[3]

That is, the dead body "enters" the earth. I don't see that the metaphor has any usefulness.

The Distances is another matter. What is happening in these poems is that the poet is speaking: they are a discourse, always beautifully modeled and beautifully constructed. The verse, by means of verse, becomes more not less expressive than speech. As, speaking of rhyme:

> let decoration thrive when
> clank is let back
> into your song.[4]

Or, if this seems like the uses of light verse:

> and who it is that sits,
> there at the base of the skull, locked
> in his throne of bone, that mere pea of bone
> where the axes meet, cross roads of the system
> god, converter, discloser, he will answer,
> will look out, if you will look, look![5]

This seems to me magnificent. But, granting once and for all that Olson is worth reading if anyone at all is worth reading, the problem remains for the reviewer and for any reader that it is impossible to confront Olson's poems without first of all acknowledging the audible presence of Pound in them. Not that Olson has not openly and handsomely acknowledged the debt to Pound in the text of the poems, but if we look to poetry as a skill by which we can grasp the form of a perception achieved, then nothing can so deaden the impact of poetic discourse as to be uncertain which of two men is speaking, to half-hear other words paralleling the words we read. It was hardly necessary to visit Mexico to write:

> And she sprinkled water on the head of the child, crying
> "Ciao-coatl! Ciao-coatl!"
> with her face to the west[6]

The link between Rapallo and the Valley of Mexico lays waste a lot of country between.[7] And in such passages as this:

>   The death in life (death itself)
> is endless, eternity
> is the false cause

The knot is other wise, each topographical corner
presents itself, and no sword
cuts it, each knot is itself a fire[8]

etc.—it goes on for several lines of rather painstaking analogy—the verse itself seems to be doing nothing. The point to be made is not that such lines as these are characteristic of Olson—they are not—but to refer again to this poet's surprising susceptibility to influence (the echo of Rilke is unmistakable in context).

But it is also true that even those poems in which one is most aware of Pound assert their own musical and intellectual life. "The Kingfishers" would attest to this, if it were not too long to quote here adequately. Perhaps these twelve lines from the fine poem *In Cold Hell, in Thicket* may give some idea of Olson's quality:

ya, selva oscura, but hell now
is not exterior, is not to be got out of, is
the coat of your own self, the beasts
emblazoned on you And who
can turn this total thing, invert
and let the ragged sleeves be seen
by any bitch or common character? Who
can endure it where it is, where the beasts are met,
where yourself is, your beloved is, where she
who is separate from you, is not separate, is not
goddess, is, as your core is,
the making of one hell[9]

Clearly one does Olson the greatest service by quoting as much as space allows. "There Was a Youth Whose Name Was Thomas Granger," which is a shattering comment on the American Theocracy, is also a demonstration of the editorial skill and the accuracy of ear which enables Olson to convert quotation into poetry. And, in fact, one could list any of the poems in this book as redounding to his credit. And yet the fact must remain that to encounter Olson's work, in spite of the currency of the phrase, is simply not an encounter with a new poetry. The question finally becomes not only how new is the voice, but how fresh therefore is the vision, and with it the materials of which the poetry makes use or which it has available to it. Perhaps we should look to such poems as "The Lordly and Isolate Satyrs," in which the voice and eye are his alone, for the best prediction of Olson's future work.

Michael McClure's *Dark Brown* is printed in a handset edition of 750 copies, according to the note on the end papers, twenty-five of which are on Alexandra Japan paper and signed by the author. The longest poem in the book—set off by a blank page facing—is a description of seven or eight successful performances of sexual acts, and contains twenty-five printings of the word *Oh,* forty-three exclamation marks, occurring singly and in clusters, and 286 words printed in capitals. Beyond displaying this very ejaculatory nature, the poem occasionally states a philosophic attitude as follows:

> . . . The muscles revolt
> each seeks to become a lover, OH STOP STOP.
> ((Pride, liberty, love have one meaning—Invention))[10]

These generalizations occur here and there. Otherwise the poems insist, as their single intention, on the state of excitement of the speaker. Only the reader's recognition of the probable excitement involved—in all of the poems, not only in the two erotic poems—can justify the exclamation marks, capitals, and typographical devices. Invariably seeking the most extreme statement, the poems display the most extreme doubt of the statement's effectiveness, turning to pure printed exclamation, a "direct" display of the writer's excitement. "I break THRU THRU THRU THRU THRU the size of any star!"[11] Similarly—not now quoting McClure—one might doubt the truth of a report seeing it written: the earth opened and the sky FELL on me! It hasn't and probably won't. This verse simply does not achieve words at all, or disperses them into excitement, intoxication, meaninglessness, a destruction of the sense of self among things. McClure has done—and said—much better things than this. From *Hymn to St. Geryon, 1* in *The New American Poetry:*

to fill out the thing as we see it!
to clothe ourselves in the action
to remove from the precious to the full swing.
To hit the object over the head. To step
into what we conjecture.[12]

The Mind's Own Place

Published in *Kulchur* 3, no. 10 (Summer 1963): 2–8; reprinted in *Montemora* 1 (Fall 1975): 132–37; also reprinted in *SP* 173–82. "The Mind's Own Place" is Oppen's most extensive essay on poetics. Originally written for *The Nation* in early 1962, the essay was rejected there, and subsequently sent for commentary to numerous correspondents, including June Oppen Degnan, Charles Humboldt, Steven Schneider, and, most significantly, Denise Levertov, "at [whose] latest poems," Oppen writes in 1962 letter to Oppen Degnan, "the thing is almost written" (*SL* 57–61). Although he received numerous suggestions, Oppen refused to revise the essay significantly. Before finding a place at *Kulchur,* Oppen considered sending it also to the *Massachusetts Review,* which had published poems of Levertov's to which Oppen had unfavorably reacted.

The title of the essay comes from Milton's *Paradise Lost* 1.250–55:

> Hail horrors, hail
> Infernal world, and thou, profoundest Hell,
> Receive thy new possessor: one who brings
> A mind not to be changed by place or time.
> The mind is its own place, and in itself
> Can make a Heaven of Hell, a Hell of Heaven.

Oppen wrote to Degnan about the title: "Milton put it in the mouth of Beelzebub, so to the Puritan Milton it is the devil's doctrine" (*SL* 380, n. 8). Oppen revisits this passage in section 7 of "A Narrative," citing as well his own essay's title:

> Serpent, Ouroboros
> Whose tail is in his mouth: he is the root
> Of evil,
> This ring worm, the devil's
> Doctrine the blind man
> Knew. His mind
> Is its own place;
> He has no story . . . (*NCP* 153; *SP* 75)

+ + +

Sargent is reported to have said to Renoir that he painted "cads in the park." And Sargent was of course quite right.[1] The passion of the Impressionists to see, and to see more clearly was a desire to see past the subject matter and the art attitudes of the academy. It is true that the artist is not dependent on his subject in the sense that he can be judged by its intrinsic interest, or that the discussion of his work can become a discussion of its subject. But the emotion which creates art is the emotion that seeks to know and to disclose. The cocoon of "Beauty" as the word is often used, the beauty of background music and of soft lights, though it might be an art, is an art of the masseur and the perfumist.

Modern American poetry begins with the determination to find the image, the thing encountered, the thing seen each day whose meaning has become the meaning and the color of our lives. Verse, which had become a rhetoric of exaggeration, of inflation, was to the modernists a skill of accuracy, of precision, a test of truth. Such an art has always to be defended against a furious and bitter Bohemia whose passion it is to assist, in the highest of high spirits, at the razing of that art which is the last intrusion on an onanism which they believe to be artistic. In these circles is elaborated a mock-admiration of the artist as a sort of super-annuated infant, and it is the nightmare of the poet or the artist to find himself wandering between the grim gray lines of the Philistines and the ramshackle emplacements of Bohemia. If he ceases to believe in the validity of his insights—the truth of what he is saying—he becomes the casualty, the only possible casualty, of that engagement. Philistia and Bohemia, never endangered by the contest, remain precisely what they were. This is the Bohemia that churns and worries the idea of the poet-not-of-this-world, the dissociated poet, the ghostly bard. If the poet is an island, this is the sea which most lovingly and intimately grinds him to sand.

There comes a time in any such discussion as this when the effort to avoid the word *reality* becomes too great a tax on the writer's agility. The word of course has long since ceased to mean anything recognizably "real" at all, but English does seem to be stuck with it. We cannot assert the poet's relation to reality, nor exhort him to face reality, nor do any of these desirable things, nor be sure that we are not insisting merely that he discuss only those things we are accustomed to talk about, unless we somehow manage to restore a meaning to the word. Bertrand Russell wrote "If I were to describe reality as I found it, I would have to include my arm."[2] In the shock of that sentence—out of context—perhaps the meaning of the word may be restored, or in the fragment of Heraclitus: "If it all went up in smoke" that smoke would remain.[3] It is the arbitrary fact, and not any quality of wisdom literature, which creates the impact of the poets. The "shock of recognition," when it is anything, is that. If we can hold the word to its meaning, or if we can import a word from elsewhere—a collective, not an abstract noun, to mean "the things that exist"—then we will not have on the one hand the demand that the poet circumstantially describe everything that we already know, and declare every belief that we already hold, nor on the other hand the ideal of the poet without any senses at all. Dante's "sweet new style" presaged a new content, a new attitude: and it was a new vision, an act of vision that ushered modern art into France, as it was an extension of awareness that forced the development of a modern poetry in this country.[4] The early moderns among painters of the United States found themselves promptly identified as the Ash Can school, and it happens that Lindsay, Sandburg, Kreymborg, Williams—the poets of the little magazine *Others* which came off a hand press in a garage somewhere in New Jersey about 1918—were almost a populist movement.[5] Though it is hard to register now, the subjects of Sandburg's poems, the stockyards and the railroad sidings, gave them their impact. Of the major poets it is only William Carlos Williams, with his insistence on "the American idiom," on the image derived from day-to-day experience, on form as "nothing more than an extension of content," who shows a derivation from populism.[6] But it is the fidelity, the clarity, including the visual clarity and their freedom from the art subject which is the distinction also of Pound and Eliot and the force behind their creation of a new form and a new prosody; the "speech rhythms" of Pound, the "prose quality" of Eliot. Their intelligence rejected the romanticism, the mere sentimental "going on" of such men as Sandburg and Kreymborg, but for them too art moves forward only when some man, or some men, get their heads above—or below—the terrible thin scratching of the art world. It is possible to find a metaphor for anything, an analogue: but the image is encountered, not found; it is an account of the poet's perception, the act of perception; it is a test of sincerity, a test of conviction, the rare poetic quality of truthfulness.[7] They meant to replace by the data of experience the accepted poetry of their time, a display by the poets of right thinking and right sentiment, a dreary waste of lies. That data was and is the core of what "modernism" restored to poetry, the sense of the poet's self among things. So much depends upon the red wheelbarrow. The distinction between a poem that shows confidence in itself and in its materials, and on the other hand a performance, a speech by the poet, is the distinction between poetry and histrionics. It is a part of the function of poetry to serve as a test of truth. It is possible to say anything in abstract prose, but a great many things one believes or would like to believe or thinks he believes will not substantiate themselves in the concrete materials of the poem. It is not to say that the poet is immune to the "real" world to say that he is not likely to find the moment, the image, in which a political generalization or any other generalization will prove its truth. Denise Levertov begins a fine poem with the words: "The authentic!" and goes on to define

> the real, the new-laid
> egg whose speckled shell
> the poet fondles and must break
> if he will be nourished

in the events of a domestic morning: the steam rising in the radiators, herself "breaking the handle of my hairbrush," and the family breakfast, to the moment when, the children being sent to school,

> cold air
> comes in at the street door.[8]

These are, as poetry intends, clear pictures of the world in verse, which means only to be clear, to be honest, to produce the realization of reality and to construct a form out of no desire for the trick of gracefulness, but in order to make it possible to grasp, to hold the insight which is the content of the poem.

T. S. Eliot's immense reputation was already established by the end of the twenties: Pound's somewhat later. It is within the present decade that Williams has achieved a comparable position. It was Eliot's influence, far more than Pound's, and Eliot's influence by way of Auden which formed the tone of the so-called Academic poets who dominated the field during the forties and early fifties, and whom the Beats assailed. It is quite possible that both Eliot and the Academic poets tend at this moment to be underrated: the Academics are perhaps suffering the difficulties of middle age. They are not Young Poets nor Old Masters, nor are they news in the exhilarating sense that they might bite a dog. But they too are not writing in complacent generalities, and the word *academic* can give a false concept of their content and form. The fact is, however, that the poets of the San Francisco school, the poets called Beat, took off not at all from Eliot, but from Pound and still more directly from Williams, and to varying degrees from Whitman, and the influence—perhaps indirect—of such men as Sandburg and Lindsay and even Kreymborg is, as a matter of fact, perfectly evident in their work. But it is to Williams that the young poets of this school acknowledge the greatest debt, and if the word *populism* applied to Williams may not be entirely justifiable, it is at any rate true that Williams is the most American of the American poets of his generation, and these young poets have been markedly and as a matter of course American.[9] I think it has been part of their strength, and in fact I fear the present pilgrimage to Japan and the exotic arms of Zen. I feel quite sure, to begin with, that Hemingway has expressed Zen to the West about as well as is likely to be done. The disciple asked: "What is Truth?" And the Master replied, "Do you smell the mountain laurel?" "Yes," said the disciple. The Master said, "There, I have kept nothing from you." What Master was that? "The archer aims not at the target but at himself."[10] Nor, as we have read, at the bull. If we are to talk of the act performed for its own sake, I think we will get more poetry out of the large fish of these waters—*even* out of the large fish in these waters—than from all the tea in Japan. But this may be because I belong to a generation that grew more American—literarily at least—as it approached adult estate: we grew up on English writing—and German fairy tales—as I think no American any longer does. Starting with Mother Goose—in the absence of "It Happened on Mulberry Street" or "Millions of Cats" or whatever has become current since my daughter grew up—and proceeding to Kipling and Robert Louis Stevenson and the Rover Boys, perhaps the only American writing we saw was in the Oz books and in Mark Twain. I have not discussed this with other writers, and risk the statement, but I believe that many a young American writer-to-be was astonished on reaching adolescence to discover that he was not easily going to take his place as the young master, or even as a Thackerayan young man who manages, with whatever difficulty, to equip himself with fresh linen and varnished boots for his crucial morning call on the Duchess. We found ourselves below stairs, possibly: certainly among the minor characters. Which was a factor I believe in our need to make our own literature. Huck Finn, if this were a scholarly work, might be contrasted to Tom Brown, or even to Christopher Robin of Pooh Corners. Alice wandered from her governess; Dorothy of Oz ran too late for the storm cellar and was caught in a Kansas cyclone. Together and contrastingly they dawned on our infant minds, and may have contributed to the aesthetic, if not social sentiment, which went in search of the common, the common experience, the life of common man. Or it may be, more simply, that the more open society made possible the literary career of the obviously non-aristocratic spokesman who, once he tired of Invocation to Someone Else's Muse, *had* to make his own poetry. I myself was not the barefoot American boy. Having been born near New York, like many of these young poets, I was undoubtedly shod by the age of three months. But neither the barefoot boy nor Robert Frost is really the most American thing in the world, and there are facts to consider beyond the orthopedic. I am constantly amazed by the English response to the Angry Young Men,[11] whose news-value appears to be that they are not of the aristocracy and are bitterly concerned with that fact in all its ramifications, whereas I have not met an American writer who had ever wondered what Vanderbilts or Morgans or Astors felt about his accent, his vocabulary, or his neckwear. Or if he wondered, he would not *know,* as the English seem to know, and the setting of Henry James's novels is to us—and even to Henry James—a curiosity, a literary paradox. And the search of the Beats, the thing which they have in common with the Ash Can school of painting and the Chicago literary renaissance of the twenties is an authentic American phenomenon, a search for the common experience, for the ground under their feet. I have strained matters considerably using the word *populist:* certainly no *more* specifically political word could be used. The poet means to trust his direct perceptions, and it is even possible that it might be useful for the country to listen, to hear evidence, to consider what indeed we have brought forth upon this continent.

The DAR is not a notably liberal organization.[12] I am aware that there must be descendents of Old Families in all possible political groupings, but a considerable portion of the population, and I think a considerable proportion of the most liberal population, is made up of the children and grandchildren and great-grandchildren of immigrants. Certainly the DAR is of that opinion. But I need not assume statistical facts which neither the DAR nor I know. The oldest families are of puritan background, and the American family histories of the descendents of later immigrants begin typically with men and women who found refuge in the tenements of these shores from political and financial shipwreck. There they developed a morality of crisis, an ethos of survival, a passionate philosophy of altruism and ambition. To a puritan morality—or I should say a puritanical morality—they added altruism in some cases, solidarity in others, and thereby completed a political morality. But neither ambition nor solidarity nor altruism is capable of establishing values. If the puritanical values proved themselves in material well-being, in the escape from danger of starvation, in TVs and radios, electric toasters and perhaps air-conditioners, electric razors and strawberry corer, and are now pushing the electric toothbrush, then altruism demands these things also for the other man. It cannot, of itself, get beyond that. We can do so only when, with whatever difficulty, with whatever sense of vertigo, we begin to speak for ourselves. Be-razored and be-toastered, and perhaps anarchist and irresponsible, the grandson of the immigrant and the descendent of the puritan better begin to speak for himself. If he is a poet he must. If he is not, perhaps he should listen. For mankind itself is an island: surely no man is a continent, and the definition of happiness must be his own.[13] The people on the Freedom Rides are both civilized and courageous; the people in the Peace Marches are the sane people of the country. But it is not a way of life, or should not be. It is a terrifying necessity. Bertolt Brecht once wrote that there are times when it can be almost a crime to write of trees. I happen to think that the statement is valid as he meant it.[14] There are situations which cannot honorably be met by art, and surely no one need fiddle precisely at the moment that the house next door is burning. If one goes on to imagine a direct call for help, then surely to refuse it would be a kind of treason to one's neighbors. Or so I think. But the bad fiddling could hardly help, and similarly the question can only be whether one intends, at a given time, to write poetry or not.[15]

It happens, though, that Brecht's statement cannot be taken literally. There is no crisis in which political poets and orators may not speak of trees, though it is more common for them, in this symbolic usage, to speak of "flowers." "We want bread *and* roses": "Let a thousand flowers bloom" on the left: on the right, the photograph once famous in Germany of Handsome Adolph sniffing the rose.[16] Flowers stand for simple and undefined human happiness and are frequently mentioned in all political circles. The actually forbidden word Brecht, of course, could not write. It would be something like *aesthetic.* But the definition of the good life is necessarily an aesthetic definition, and the mere fact of democracy has not formulated it, nor, if it is achieved, will the mere fact of an extension of democracy, though I do not mean of course that restriction would do better. Suffering can be recognized; to argue its definition is an evasion, a contemptible thing. But the good life, the thing wanted for itself, the aesthetic, will be defined outside of anybody's politics, or defined wrongly. William Stafford ends a poem titled "Vocation" (he is speaking of the poet's vocation) with the line: "Your job is to find what the world is trying to be."[17] And though it may be presumptuous in a man elected to nothing at all, the poet does undertake just about that, certainly nothing less, and the younger poets' judgment of society is, in the words of Robert Duncan, "I mean, of course, that happiness itself is a forest in which we are bewildered, turn wild, or dwell like Robin Hood, outlawed and at home."[18]

It is possible that a world without art is simply and flatly uninhabitable, and the poet's business is not to use verse as an advanced form of rhetoric, nor to seek to give to political statements the aura of eternal truth. It should not really be the ambition even of the most well-meaning of political and semipolitical gatherings to do so, and to use verse for the purpose, as everyone perfectly well knows, is merely excruciating. Therefore the poet, speaking as a poet, declares his political nonavailability as clearly as the classic pronouncement: "If nominated I will run: if elected I will hide" (I quote from memory).[19] Surely what we need is a "redemption of the will"—the phrase from a not-yet-produced young playwright whose work I have read—and indeed we will not last very long if we do not get it. But what we must have *now,* the political thing we must have, is a peace. And a peace is made by a peace treaty. And we have seen peace treaties before; we know what they are. This one will be, if we get it, if we survive, like those before it, a cynical and brutal division of the world between the great powers. Everyone knows what must be in that document: the language of both sides has been euphemistic but clear. A free hand in Eastern Europe to Russia: to the United States in Western Europe and in this continent and some other places. And the hope that China will not soon acquire a bomb. And where is the poet who will write that she opened her front door, having sent the children to school, and felt the fresh authentic air in her face and wanted—*that?*

A Review of David Antin's *Definitions*

Published in *Elizabeth* 12 (November 1968): 35. Untitled review of David Antin, *Definitions* (New York: Caterpillar Press, 1967).

+ + +

These poems are definitions of the present and a response to the present. Pity, the tremendous awareness of pity, is here the one impulse the poems permit themselves toward exhortation, toward the enunciation of demands; the poems confront the world at the precise edge of the intellectual present, the precise point of the instructed mind.

The world is seen here in the intellectual structures which are a present truth. Impossible to see beyond these formal expressions, impossible to recognize less than the mind has now publicly touched. The absence of a dead friend, the presence of that friend in the past expressed in the immaterial axioms of time and space; yet thirst is a reality, grief is a reality, neither thirst nor grief is assuaged. Our thirst and our grief, and our cruelty, existing among immaterial concepts, immaterial axioms, insistent koans which formulate the present in reasonable lines arriving again and again at the impossible, the inacceptable, the mind moving outward continually into areas in which we cannot live, the poems reaching their poetic achievement in a definition of the student's present.

Encountering the imprint of a small press, one deals again with the term *avant-garde*. Understood as referring not to exiled groups but to the heart of the matter, the term may regain a meaning in application to these supple poems. The format of the book, which suggests a student's note-book, is, for the occasion, the perfect design, a brilliantly made book.

On Armand Schwerner

Published in *Stony Brook* 3–4 (1969): 72. Review of Armand Schwerner, *Seaweed* (Santa Barbara, CA: Black Sparrow Press, 1969). The quotation from his own work that Oppen mentions is from his poem "A Narrative" (*NCP* 150; *SP* 72), and appears in the first section of Schwerner's "prologue in six parts" (the poem from which Oppen quotes twice here). Oppen comments on and critiques the poem in an August 1964 letter to Schwerner (*SL* 101–2), and mentions it in Daybook II: III, noting in the latter that Schwerner is comparing him to Akiba, and suggesting that Oppen understood the passage quoted here as addressed, at least partly, to himself.

+ + +

Surely adequate diatribes have been launched against the critical vocation and the public; everyone is pleasingly terrified, a terror rapidly increasing, and the early-baronial force of a Pound when imitated, becomes a display of competitive bullying. Moreover, time passes and one watches things work out fairly reasonably, reputations withered and reputations made. But these mills do grind abominably slowly and a poet may wait a decade or two to be spoken of at all, then to be spoken of timidly by portmanteau reviewers disturbed by lacking a precedent for praise. To touch on a number of "schools," there are, for example, Harvey Shapiro and William Bronk, there is, for example, Armand Schwerner,

> hungry and sleeping in caves all winter, in summer
> returning on time for the leaves, no
> counting of steps, mostly, most
> memorably, marked most by this giving
> birth[1]

Does anyone know anything finer than this?

> Akiba, angel of the will, teach me
> how to listen, the stance a little down, the proper
> movement toward the bare ground, a return

alive, the keeping of a name
by the satisfactions of a regular breathing
not utterly drowned in common air [2]

Why—asked quietly, but why—must Schwerner appear now, in his most complete presentation to date, in an edition limited to 750 copies? It would seem to be pure chance, critical law asserting itself, at best, in inverse ratio to the chances of a poet's having survived long enough to benefit by it. Again:

But
did you listen to their hearts, did you
put your mouth to their wet mouths
and give them air?

No.
Then perhaps one of them was alive [3]

A number of experimental poems, largely experiments in the isolation of words, a radical exploration, depend on space and the organization of the page which cannot be displayed in brief quotation but achieve in the book a remarkably pure lyricism of word and silence and of skepticism. There appears a quotation from my work in one of the longer poems, but some community of interest and of sensitivity will be assumed, I hope, without suggesting the prior existence of cliques. I risk it in any case: one begins to fear that poets of worth may be lost in the impenetrable welter of publication as once they were lost in general neglect. I think there should be recognized in these poems the presence of a lyric poet of depth and delicacy and power. I think, moreover, that these qualities and song itself, whatever one may read in reviews, are very rare indeed.

A Note on Tom McGrath etc.

First published in *West End* 1, no. 2 (Summer 1972): 10–11; reprinted in *Ironwood* 5 (1975): 42. Thomas McGrath (1916–90) was a poet, leftist activist, pamphleteer, founding editor of *Crazy Horse,* and editor, with Charles Humboldt (1910–64), of *Masses and Mainstream.* McGrath was blacklisted from his teaching job at Los Angeles State University by Joseph McCarthy's House Un-American Activities Committee in 1953. Among his works is the long poem *Letters to an Imaginary Friend.*

+ + +

> Thomas Merton: "In the continual *vroom vroom vroom* of the guitars we must learn a new kind of stubbornness." And further Rilke: "the arts that copulate and copulate and never conceive."

It is the sympathy, the human universe, and the nightmare vision of the decadent arts that move some poets toward the Left and its moralities. Thomas McGrath was among those poets whose concern for the product of his art seemed to the Old Left to be in itself an impermissible heterodoxy, while those untouched by the Left, unable to credit a moral passion, regarded him as "a poet in uniform." A review published in the late fifties reported that a book of his contained the word *proletarian,* and bothered to say no more, while still broader and less knowing strata of the reading public encountered in his work concerns with which they were unfamiliar and experiences which they had not shared, and found him merely incomprehensible.

No need of detail. Why detail it now? We will become involved in an effort to display to the present and admirable young—the all-but wholly admirable young—that as they enter a struggle in which lives are at stake they are drawn into an orgy of death or into an exclusively moral judgment of art that demands that one say what one wishes to be said, that one believe what one wishes to believe. Nor can we find the strength to condemn this. It can be observed—and Jacques Maritain has said it clearly and at length—that when we say "moral" we mean that which concerns the destiny of humanity. That destiny is now so profoundly in question that contemplation and the modes of art, the love of the intellect for what exists, the longing of the intellect for all that exists, begins again to give way to other modes. One makes his own decision. And McGrath, who feels himself so close to the Irish Bards, as he defiantly told the House Un-American Activities Committee, must again take his chances.

Possessed of his own stubbornness in his own time—gift perhaps as he believes of the Irish Bards—Tom has no need of my comment. I would want in some way to dedicate this inadequate note to Joe Hecht, to Charles Humboldt, to Sidney Finkelstein, less stubborn and beyond recall, and to many others, I do not know how many.[1]

A Letter

Published in *Agenda* 11, nos. 2–3 (1973): 58–59. A response to a questionnaire sent to poets by *Agenda* editors William Cookson and Peter Dale: "The purpose of [the] questionnaire is to seek practical answer [*sic*] from poets concerning their methods and intentions in their disposition of their poems upon the page. We are not investigating the absolute nature of rhythm so much as the rhythmic intention behind the print. Because of the variety of rhythmic systems, numbers of questions may seem irrelevant to your practice. Please ignore these and treat the questionnaire as a guide; we would prefer to a straightforward account of your practice in continuous prose" (38). The questionnaire as a whole is longer than Oppen's response. The two questions to which he seems to be most directly responding are: "1. Apart from obvious differences, such as of accent on words like 'temporary' and 'civilization', do you recognize in your work a distinction between English and American sufficient to entail new systems of rhythm or metre?" and "8. Are you conscious, like Eliot, of a constant approach towards and retreat from some norm? If so, what are your usual norms?"

As upon initial publication, anomalous typography and spacing are preserved.

+ + +

I answer your questions in shorthand not because they seem to me uninteresting or unimportant, but for the contrary reasons, and I am deeply in work at the moment and must try to remain on the surface or to hold my distance. I'll follow, here, the order in which the questions are asked—or more or less that order.

The problem of English vs. American accent. Yes, it troubles me, nor is this all: there are local accents in both countries heard a young man reading in the state of Maine, reading Pope: his voice carried no implication, no trace of iambic, and he was not aware of the possibility of that scansion—

it was, in fact, not possible for him. AND the American South—not to mention the unimagined cadences of the Beatles—who could have foreseen them?—

like others, I have pondered notations——I know of none that offer a solution to this problem. (it might be well to consider Eliot's extraordinary capacity to echo voices in the Waste Land—(yes, I meant: voices *in the waste land* but the voice that leaps, the voice that leaps outward

outward   up ward?

—and so, indeed, one speaks to himself. The process by which sometimes a line is found, I cannot trace. Given a line, one has a place to stand   And go further

from Song: The Winds of Downhill

. . . Who

so poor the words

would   *with and*   take on substantial

meanings   handholds   footholds

to dig in one's heels   sliding

hands and heels beyond the residential
lots   the plots   it is a poem

which may be sung
may well be sung[1]

i.e.: there are "accents" which are WRONG. We, the poets, change the accents, change the speech. We change the speech because we are not explaining, agitating, convincing: we do not write what we already knew before we wrote the poem.[2]

I think I've answered.

Untitled: ". . . will"

First published in *The Four Zoas* 1 (1974), not paginated. Typographical anomalies are retained.

+ + +

. . . will
played out against the poem
relates, could relate to the
Objectivist Sincerity and Objectification! Stronger
I think more useful *now* than that objectivist formulation.
The will and the poem.
AND the mystery of the "will"
(and) elsewhere To rid the poem of impositions, false
impositions: to trust the *content*. To speak as clearly
as it can of TIME. *A* TIME
if word *A* must be next to word *B,* GET it there.
This is what revision *is*
the Language is not a gift, a
request, ready wrapped and with an owner's manual, a set
of dashboard instructions or something to say to the service-
station attendant: you must know what you're doing, what's
happening in "the works" because they're yours
These are hasty notes I mean to speak only of the way
to proceed further or what would, for me, be the way
to do so
Some notes, in their haste, in the form of assertions.
Add question marks where decency and modesty would wear them
I would only add, with deliberate assertiveness: this is
what revision *is*

Non-Resistance, etc. Or: Of the Guiltless

Published in *West End* 3, no. 1 (Summer 1974): 5. Oppen's meditation on his decision to join the war effort against Hitler. He was inducted in the army in November 1942, and served with the 411th Infantry in the 103rd Division.

+ + +

If I did not resist a force—a force such as the force of Hitler—a force that would exterminate almost all those I knew, friends, daughter, Mary, nieces, grand-nieces, grand-nephews, radicals, liberals, the poets-

If I fought, and fought to kill, I would suffer guilt, the guilt of guilt AND the guilt of fear, the desire to run, the guilt that I've told of, the guilt of that foxhole (and who does fight? The deceived, the idiot, the stupid and also those with no choice, those who must be heroes to refuse the crime)[1]

If I killed, I would suffer guilt. If I did not, I would suffer . . . I don't even know a word, a name for what I would suffer

—that I did not exist and never had, the terrible knowledge of a fake, a lie, that nothing had been as I said, pretended, that I had loved no one, that those who had loved me or anyone like me had deceived themselves, pitifully, tragically had deceived themselves, had drawn the simplest, delusory mere warmth from my presence, had been deceived, betrayed, demeaned, had given all they could give for nothing, to nothing, had been nothing—In the last moments they would know this. Die like me, or fight with nothing, without what they had thought was themselves, without a past, with nothing. Thrown away, unloved, shamed, degraded

—stripped naked, herded into the gas ovens. *Think*

Think also of children. The guards laughing.

Yes, we deceive ourselves   Better, we say, to aim a rifle at an unknown man and pull the trigger. Carefully, if we can   Or release bombs from the air. He, like us (he, the target) has "his own" army, the children will display the medals   We deceive ourselves with these things, but the other? We cannot do it   The children cannot die alone. There must have been a father, a mother, there must have been friends, there must have been *someone*.

Statement on Poetics

First published posthumously in *Sagetrieb* 3, no. 3 (Winter 1984): 25–27. Prior to interviewing Oppen on May 1, 1975, Reinhold Schiffer sent him a letter querying him about his prosody. The "Statement on Poetics" is Oppen's reply. The interview took place in the Oppens' home on Polk Street, San Francisco, and was later published with the "Statement" in the same issue of *Sagetrieb* (10–23). Kathryn Shevelow, editor of the issue's special section on Oppen, added the following note vis-à-vis the "Statement": "The typescript of the manuscript breaks off [at the end] without a period. In the Schiffer interview, GO quotes from the 'Statement,' and the passage he quotes does not appear in this typescript. Thus it would appear that some part of the manuscript of the 'Statement' has been lost" (27).

+ + +

Let me just make a start—and then we'll come to the questions.

You've asked me to discuss the "prosody" of the poems, feeling that discussions of my work have concentrated too much on what might be called a philosophy that they express. Of course, the two cannot be very clearly distinguished, but I will address myself to the *process* of writing the poem, and I will do so as clearly as I can. Duncan somewhere says, "The feeling of presence, not concept." And I too have felt this necessity. In *Discrete Series* is a poem called "Drawing" which contains the lines:

> the paper, turned, contains
> This entire volume (*NCP* 33)

This is to say the same thing that Duncan has said—the drawing as simultaneous music, as the poem must also be—the statement and the modulations and the music all come from the same well. That simultaneity cannot be prescribed, of course, it must be found.

I, surely, cannot hope to prescribe. I try one word and another word and another word, reverse the sequence, alter the line-endings, a hundred two hundred rewritings, revisions—This is called prosody: how to write a poem. Or rather, how to write *that* poem. I'll read a few lines of my poem "Escape":

Escape
love like the shining of rails in the night
the shining way the way away
from home arrow in the air
hat-brim fluttering in the wind as she runs
forward and it seemed to me so beautiful so beautiful
the sun-lit air it was no dream all's wild
out there as we unlikely
image of love found the way
away from home[1]

Should the word be "seemed"? Or should it be "seems"? Is the past more vivid? Or is the past raised into the present, the past *present* in the present? It is not a matter of syntax alone: the *s* of seems brings the line into the present—it seemed to me that the *d* of seemed was needed there, whatever the "story," the line of the story may be, that stop of the *d* must be there—that stop which might be revealment. All speaks, when it speaks, in its own shape. I do not know why. Perhaps we may call it music. The word, the right word, it seems to stand outside of us—like the shining of rails in the night, and even the way away from home. I suppose it is music. There is a mystery: the mystery is that the ear knows. If one revises and revises and revises—perhaps weeks and months and years and cannot revise, then there is something wrong with what you are trying to say. The ear knows, and I don't know why. It is, perhaps, partly as we hear it in the voice—no matter how one attempts to manipulate his voice. All must speak, and speak in its own voice—every "and" and "but"—the word *is*—The word in one's own mouth becomes as strange as infinity—even as strange as the finite, strange as things. Primarily and above all and note by note the prosody carries the relation of things and the sequence: the poet learns almost everything from his own verse, his own prosody.

It is true that my own temperament, my own sense of drama, enters into this: I like to seem to be speaking very simply—and a sense of drama is dangerous, I know that, this is again a question of modulation, as is music: a question of honesty, question of sincerity—the sincerity of the *I* and the *we,* it is a tremendous drama, the things that common words say, the words "and" and "but" and "is" and "before" and "after." Our true faith is said in the simple words, for we cannot escape them—for meaning is the instant of meaning—and this means that we write to find what we believe and what we do not believe: there are things we believe or want to believe or think we believe that will not substantiate themselves in the concrete materials of the poem—I've said before—.[2] And that's prosody, it is a music but it is a rigorous music—a music that refuses all trumpets, all sweet harmonies, all lusts and emotions that aren't there, it is a music, quite simply, of image and honest speech—*image* because image is the moment of conviction. It cannot be altered and it cannot be falsified without one's knowing it. Prosody is a language, but it is a language that tests itself. Or it tests itself in music—I think one may say that. It tests the relations of things: it carries the sequence of disclosure. And that is its vividness. More vivid than falsification, a test of conviction, the sequence of disclosure. I am not speaking of a philosophic naiveté, I am not speaking of kicking the rock and saying By God, sir, that's *here,* and certainly I'm not speaking of any remarkable philosophic sophistication. I am thinking of *actualness,* not some toughness of "realism," some manly toughness: I am talking of consciousness—which is to say, I am talking of experience, and THAT is to say, I am talking of emotion. Impossible to doubt the actualness of one's own consciousness: but therefore consciousness in itself, of itself, by itself carries the principle of ACTUALNESS for it, itself, is actual beyond doubt.

And actualness is prosody, it is the purpose of prosody and its achievement, the instant of meaning, the achievement of meaning and of *presence,* the sequence of disclosure which comes from everywhere; life-style, angers, rebellions—I am not apolitical, and it is possible to mock poetry, it is certainly possible to mock poetry just as there are times when one is sick of himself, but eventually, I think, there is no hope for us but in meaning. For Voltaire was wrong you know: anything can be said, there is a great deal too foolish to be sung.[3] Those who merely chatter await an interruption that will save them from themselves. Which means again that the prosody and the "philosophy" cannot be separated as of course you know—but I can speak primarily of the process of poetry, and poetry has come from everywhere: life-style, rebellion, anger and happiness and everything we know or think we know.

Daybooks

The noise of wealth, the clamor of wealth
In the hotel lobby sound, ~~more than~~ hardship
Like the voice of Hell.

The dream

Truth ~~follows~~ must follow
after things

Nevertheless, truth follows
The existance of something

[Eliphas Levi: "an eternity of isolation would be eternal death"]

14
18
18
34.5
620
14
80
72
0

Balzac — Seraphita f[illegible] [illegible]
Swimme Wart
Leviathan
"The hysterical of bric-a-brac" "[illegible]"
1 2 3 4 5 6 7 8
2 4 6 8 10 12 14 16
deluge of

Beyond
IF NOT this bric-a-brac, NOTHING

Daybook I

The entirety of Oppen's "Stapled Daybook," an unsequenced series of papers stapled together by Oppen ca. 1963–64. References to Mexico in some excised writings, as well as letterhead with the Oppens' Mexican address, open the possibility that some of these papers were composed before the family permanently returned to the United States in January 1960. According to Linda Oppen, however, a large portion of letterhead survived the Oppens' trip back to the States, so there is no certainty as to the date of composition. Oppen's opening reference here to Herbert Biberman's blacklisted film *Salt of the Earth* (see note 1) nevertheless remains intriguing in this regard. Drafts of poems later included in *The Materials, This in Which,* and *Of Being Numerous* are among excisions. Also excised are personal notes, drafts of letters (sent and unsent), illegible writings, and poem drafts.

+ + +

"real proletarian," "salt of the earth," etc.[1]

The people in the capitalist countries have only a theoretical ^*and formal*^ right to elect the government, whereas the Socialist governments possess a real and effective right to elect the people.

—childish self-pity leading merely to idiotic reactionary attitudes.

The 60 generations of historical time—We are an old race: that is, there have been alot of us.
That must face age

We feel it was ourselves who live through history. No other people do?—The orphan blitheness of "others"

Words are a constant enemy: the thing seems to exist because the word does[2]

The assistant, the suppliers, the managements:

The iron ships in the harbor, the iron locomotives at the
the edge of the city:

The black pilings driven into the sea's bottom, the
divers, the pilings gathering sea growth in the
disturbed harbor-water

The light of an office window shining on the window ledge
of snow

(Inert? Inert poetry? Inert steel?)

—never really touches the bases of life at all. He actually touches only attitudes, affections, poses, styles—[3]

The "public feeling"—not primarily self expression, tho the word is a refuge. But to add something to literature. The fear it might never be said.

Whatever I write has already
happened—at least to me.

We will return to this place?

The old people gather
Tastelessly in a room which is the old country
bragging of the grandchildren . . .

+ + +

The courage of clarity.

Intrepidly clear.

For each particle of oxygen,
two of hydrogen—

for this the ship floats,
for this the man drowns
The wind and the eyes,
of the same particle (cf louis)[4]

Oriental art: the thing and its distinction
(which of course reveals actually the human
subjectivity: human meanings)

+ + +

There is the area of Lyric—the
area in which one is absolutely
convinced that one's emotions
are an insight into reality
and death
But values—as they say—

+ + +

The noise of wealth, the clamour of wealth[5]
In the hotel lobby sound ~~more than hardship~~

Like the voice of Hell.

<u>*the dream*</u>

Truth ~~follows~~ must follow
after things

Nevertheless, Truth follows
The existence of <u>something</u>[6]

[Eliphas Levi "an eternity of isolation]
[would be eternal death"[7]]

Balzac— Seraphita, Louis Lambert[8]
Simone Weil
Leviathan[9]
"a nightmare of bric-a-brac" *Miller*[10]

1 2 3 4 5 6 7 8 - - - - - - - -
2 4 6 8 10 12 14 16

beyond
IF NOT this ^deluge of^ bric-a-brac, Nothing[11]

+ + +

I don't think life should be valued only when it can be sentimentalized (this remark derived from Yeats)

—even Keats feeling that he had to say something "profound"—Keats weakening —writes Beauty is truth truth beauty—If it were true, the line would be beautiful, and it is not.[12] It is not in any case how poetry makes "meaning" The meaning of Williams' poetry, for example, is that life is not valuable only when it can be sentimentalized or only when it can be generalized. To be able to say that, as I have said it here, does not constitute great poetry, of course; the achievement of the poet is to prove it by the aesthetic success of the poem. And Williams' vision——— . . .

and Williams has been important to us: the end of sentiment, the end of generalization is very nearly upon us: it is no longer convincing. Williams therefore
/ . . .

the thread of generalization

+ + +

What Snow and Swenson are describing is—a classic.[13]

It can not be said that Rezi was as "important" as Williams, Pound, Eliot, because he was not important in the development of modern poetry. Simple, almost none of the poets had read him. He could have been of great importance, it is even true that it would have been a very good thing if he had played an important role: he would have presented at least an alternative to the influence of Williams, the aridities derived from Eliot—We might have avoided a great many difficulties; Williams' model has rather made fakery easy, Pound

and the obfuscations of Ezra Pound

invite even easier imitation, and tho Auden and the Eliot school are perhaps not altogether easy to imitate, it is at least true that the manner apparently can be acquired with a certain amount of education even by those ~~with no~~ ^*who possess no*^ poetic intuition at all.

but it is probable that nothing of
importance in Rezi can be imitated. And it is likely that
which explains the neglect of his work

+ + +

Paz's poem— Exact or example is not a real opposite to Ambiguous.[14]

The poem is opaque. He is stating facts which refer back to the things I already know, which never exist in the poem. "Wounds"—because, yes, a word makes a mark, a wound, it impresses itself. "Effulgent" because it illuminates, yes. Those are things I know about words. But there is no place in that poem for the wound, there is no scene in which the effulgence takes place. It is just something I too understand. So that he is saying only "me too," which is the very ~~heart~~ ^*sign*^ of Provincial poetry.

he knows, or thinks he knows, from Rimbaud that such things can be done, but the poem does not earn the right to do it. The words are not really opposited, therefore the whole weight falls on the word But, so that it ~~becomes~~ merely a grammatic contraption . . . *in which nothing actually happens. The poet feels it to happen with a "but"*

+ + +

At least two kinds of devotion. The devotion to art, a sort of pragmatism of art which refuses to think anything which will not contribute to poetry. The other is a devotion which ~~tries to~~ makes poetry of what the mind, the free and operating mind ~~thinks~~ *can know—~~or must~~ know—and is going to know.*

Before horror, everything.
Beyond horror, nothing.

O scow or barge loose —should safely be moored. But people, those people who have power in them?

Who could have imagined two or three hundred years ago that the whole mass of the population would prove capable of filling out tax returns, paying bills, obtaining licenses, etc.

The advantage of NY—one is perfectly sure that it exists, because it is brutally ugly.[15]

The thing and its distinction; the quality of the walnut shell.

As human history accumulates the people come to see "the world as a limited whole" That vision has no answer to it. Perhaps it is lethal.

The product of rhetoric

Those who do not attempt to write, who have not written anything down, like those who do only mental arithmetic have not carried the processes very far

The pop art—a Disneyland tour of Dadism? or the anger, the destructiveness of the homosexual, the totally disconnected, the man without natural valences—to him not only the structure but the purposes of society must seem AT ALL MOMENTS totally absurd

A cultural game? Genet's cultural game?[16]

A noisy thinker. Who must always think badly.

"Pilgrimages and churches have always made me cry, and there, at Chalma, almost all those who reached the church door were crying"
Children of Sanchez, Marta speaking[17]
The pilgrims; companionship.

"For example; my aunt is not going to last much longer,
page 317

The very large hills, and the small coves at their feet.

The woods: non-historic time. But New England? Or "the English in Virginia"?[18]

+ + +

If, in a poor country, a primitive country, someone suggested: Let us hold a raffle, and thru a system of tokens, or in some other way give to a few individuals the right to use the labor of hundreds or even thousands so that at least someone among us will be able really to taste life, to the see the world, perhaps to report on it, to enjoy love without stint, to read and to think, and to exhaust the possibilities of adventure and of pleasure—if someone suggested that in a hopeless country, I think I would be tempted to agree. But actually, those who are able to claim the product of others' labor see nothing, learn nothing, feel nothing, are pre-occupied almost continually with the attempt to avoid discomfort, at which somehow they fail. ~~They appear to read little and to think not at all, love is no more prevalent among them than among the poorest~~ The princess suffers agonies because there is a lump in the bed; the millionairess nearly dies because the plane was not adequately heated.

+ + +

a friend of Mary's who is an etcher—Ponce deLeon—speaks of depths of focus in a picture.[19] It is among other~~s~~ things, he says, the relation of the artist to the "thing." The concept can be applied also to writing; a style can be too much on the surface. It can also be too little on the surface, the thing behind it can lack immediacy, can lack ~~light~~ *conviction.*

You can find this depth controlled perfectly in some of Joyce, in Ginsberg's Kaddish. And *somewhat* less than perfectly in Virginia Woolf. And, to make it obvious, in Corso, etc.

+ + +

The great paved places
Of France: Father? Father?[20] Distant America
Is not worth thinking of:
Is not worth thinking of

Scept that nothing else matters
        defined by defining everything which it is not

Humanism: Because people exist. What other things exist?

        America, which we did not find,
Tho we went in search of it.

        across the plains. A ship moored off France is
What? less bleakly moored?
                                        And pluck from this thistle
                                        The mirabelle!
napoleonic building, a wealth
of heavy ancestry
Brutally holds the common stone
Of the fields, more brutal for the fluted peristyle
The villages; nature not conquered
The dead are not here, even at the simple meals
as elsewhere, the dead are not here (the meals, family
meals, to which therefore they seem to have a right)

                                nothing explained by newtonian mechanics.[21]
        the arrow of time ~~which pierces nothing~~ *BLUNTED*
the most simple
Is the body of god
What will we know, discover? The grains?
The particles? The thing was here, the whole thing. It's
elaboration in the boulevards, etc.
The mineral, which is a bout as far as you can go[22]
skilled in their little city
                        the courage of clear speech

I thought once that given a decent enough life, wealth enough, for everyone, we would eventually undertake as equals to face and to reconcile ourselves to everything—well, just in the knowledge of human happiness

I know of no hope but companionship, and there cannot be companionship with people who have admitted nothing—

the little amoeba at the heart of things   a god
        is male or female
                        —the wonder of greed—
What have I to do with 6th ave, what has anyone to do with it?

The things <u>*don't*</u> *know their names*

The truth shall make us free! The lies shall make it possible to live.[23]

This culture belongs to us -- the poets, artists, prfessors, sciebtists Intellectuals -- precisey as it always has, xxxxxxxxxxxx The things we say, the complains we make agai st the world represent the innermost nature of our culture, its most basic beliefs and its fundamental values. The teen age gangs who attack people in the parks and t e streets with tire chains, and the older failures who are gathering in the John Birch society are those to whom the roles provided by the culture are inaccessible, they want, if they could, to fight a revolution against those who

who are not able to play any of the roles which have been defined as meanigful by our culture, What they want is to overthrow us who are pre-empting the meanignful roles, the lives which have meaning/within/this/culture// as meaning is defined by this culture.

It so happens that I well, happen to occupy a position at the precise apex of the pyrmaid; there is no one who outranks me. First, because I am a poet, which is a which gives me a position somewhere in the upper layers of the cultural pyrmad, and finnally because I am an unknown and undiscovered poet, which plazes me at the highest position of our societ. I outrank the President of the United States. It is undertsnssthat if the President had the temerity to i nvite me for dinner, I would contempruously refuse. If I did not refuse, I would no longer be an unknown poet, of course, and I would no longer outrank the President.

those who have not been granted a role defined as meanigful by this culture, and who lead, therefore, lives without meaning and without drama ahd without honor.

What they want, what they so violently and deangerously want, is a revolution which will overthrow us who are prempting the meanigful roles in this society.

(ADDED IN 1969: They want a redistribution of meaningful ROLES))

Daybook II:I

Part 1 of the first "Pipe-Stem Daybook," papers bound by Oppen into a small makeshift book by means of pipe-stem cleaners (ca. 1966). This Daybook is divided into five parts, one for each folder in the archive. The reasons for the archival divisions of some of Oppen's Daybooks into separate folders are not entirely clear, although these divisions do provide a useful means of organization. I have retained them here for this reason. Excisions include poem-drafts (the majority of them having to do with poems later included in *This in Which*), a few drafts of letters, and illegible and ephemeral writings. The majority of these writings were likely produced in 1962–65, although notes suggest that Oppen returned to and revised certain pages and passages as late as 1969.

+ + +

socialism—one can say its a better economic system if he thinks it is. But cannot go on arguing with artists in the name of socialism, or murdering the class enemy, or inventing apocalyptic theories—

and—There are people oppressed, people suffering, a man besieged, a man in a burning building. What precisely is established if I sacrifice my life for his?[1]

Millions of young people in this country today have grown up without experience in poverty. If one tells them of the thirties they agree that such things are abominable. But what have we to say to <u>them</u>?

As per Bronk: *agreed we are others, we are members of one another, and therefore we are alone.*[2]

there is nobody here but us.

He thrust his chin forward, trying not to cry, and the light caught his raised face, the eyes still blind with drink—[3]

Those terrible cities
Of heavy industry
"Like a blow in the chest"
Lonely and endless
Beyond speech—

(ashamed of bulk, of thought,
Of being, of eating)

Sybaon;   the fleatus of the narrow escape

My objection to being aristocratic is that I am more evangelical than aristocratic

The things people do, June, the things   people   do[4]

The man unable to distinguish the subjective from the objective is capable of fanaticism, but not of an ethic.

has lost the primary awareness, the awareness of being

+ + +

On the lady poets—women generally see no purpose in life or in art other than to make things which will contribute to happiness—at the least, to comfort. I see no purpose, or I am not sure what the purpose is, in saying terrible things.

They mean to sit near people, when they are ill, and comfort them——until the end.[5]

I can't tell people what i think

Because some people wrote a book a long time ago, ~~they~~ *many* think they know what God is

Impossible to use a word without finally wondering what one means by it. I would find that I mean nothing, that everything remained precisely as it was without the word, or else that I am naming absolute implausibilities, which are moreover the worst of all nightmares

We die we die we die

~~All there is to say~~

The sea anemone dreamed of something

No reason he should not

Or each one does

Filtering the sea water thru his body.

trinity; the man, the spirit, and the mystery.
Which is man. And says nothing about god.

an inconceivably brutal universe; it is possible
that sea anemones dream continually

absolutely unintelligible universe   to make itself human; it is possible that sea anemones dream continually[6]

+ + +

A dying class, having begun to accept the responsibilities of an aristocracy, threatens to be destroyed almost as soon as it has been born

A very old and very secure ruling class tends inevitably to be concerned with the atmosphere of life within the country which it rules. A rising class, a class becoming rich, is concerned only with the conquest of wealth for itself.

+ + +

A hypnotic art, ~~magic art~~, a dithyrambic art protected by its special vocabulary, etc——It produces such a destitute world, such a destroyed world, when that music stops, precisely like the[7]

I do not easily give myself to such things. I do not insist on knowing who's my papa, who's my mama, and whom I love, but I do ^*very much*^ want to know—while we live—which is north and which is south, *where the ground is, and where it ends*

Door—meaning a common door, with a door knob—& panels

Shapiro; able almost to leap beyond the current fashion as he was able almost to leap beyond the Auden style—But American? What language is this: "Poem condemned to wear black, be quoted in churches, versatile as Greek. Condemned to remain unsung by criminals."[8]

This attack and self confession less meaningful than my "limits of life"[9]

The popular strategy of insult!   [   ] given sophistication by the art of Hari Kari, evades responsibility by begging for execution—

French: and the persistent weakness, the root weakness of French poetry <u>and</u> French prose

\+ + +

The French Moderns—merely abominable poetry, to state it briefly

they believe they can throw words into the poem, stringing them on the most ordinary syntactical structure, and with the words they believe   and they believe the words will fill the poem with meaning. But words of themselves carry only the most conventional, that is, the most generalized meanings. It is necessary   It is the purpose

It is the proper purpose, or the first purpose of the poem to restore the meaning of words.

the generalized meaning, the mere color and "suggestiveness" of words absolves the poet of responsibility, and protects him from censure.

"The red train climbs the hill"
a questionable sentence

+ + +

Rene Char etc

I do not think that a poem can be filled with meaning by being filled, like a bag or a jug, with words. On the contrary is the poem, the structure of meaning which restores the words to clarity. The word is the burden, the words are the burden, of the line which it must ~~bear~~ ^*lift*^ up into meaning

Nor is it true that the words are chosen with honesty. Such words as Queen and King, such words as fressonne, ardent, column, fragile—the poems lean on such words, the poems move exclusively in such words—they have no other force.[10]

+ + +

that funny little core of myself which seems always so inartistic—as it must, because it is that part of any other artist——The aesthete has convinced himself—or more often herself—that the core is the appreciation of Chinese vases, or—whatever. If one remembers that he was once a four year old————[11]

Not of course Freudian investigations—not the sense of the self, the sense of the not-self. The sea, for instance—or the front yard—

The New Yorker: I suppose I exaggerate. Such that I do like to be indexed. And the ads are pretty hard to bear. I don't really write to appear between Bikini bras & Gruen watches.

I just don't really want to have anything to do with it. And don't have anything to do with it.

I look out my window, the last thing I can think about is the New Yorker:

Esquire seems likely to replace it— it is simply so god damn SILLY!

Is it a good thing? We want a kind of immortality to continue, or a kind of immortality for ourselves. But isn't it asking a good deal? A great deal of suffering, in order to remember us[12]

+ + +

Lawson on Miller:[13]
A strange passion. He is so much an athlete of virtue. Or perhaps gladiatorial rather than virtuous. As politicians, such people are surely the most to be respected, surely to be respected in contrast to the democratic conventions, say, which is a carnival, and in fact a humiliating event. Their position is truly extreme, and has therefore a kind of grandeur; they mean no less than that each man should regard his life as a part of every other man's life.

Actually, of course, I have only one life, and that my own. I would not want to insist on it to Lawson and thereby destroy his athleticism, but—he has only one life. He would find "the theater of the absurd" less a "papier mache world" if he came to realize that. It is, after all, the fact.

These are not meditations; they are deliberate efforts of affirmation. And it has affirmed too little about almost nothing "as if a snail should"—the Bronk lines[14]

Cid and Louis: some create meaning and some have meaning thrust upon them.[15]

The J H L's are fine enough people, but they are people who long long ago somehow acquired the vocation of arguing with artists.[16] They happen to be color-blind, tone deaf.
Form blind, the writers of ~~class movies and class plays~~ ^*Hollywood movies or Broadway plays or intolerable novels*^ to begin with, and art is meaningless to them. Therefore they have been patiently pointing

out for forty years that art should not be meaningless. They are right, of course . . .

+ + +

This culture belongs to us—the poets, artists, professors, scientists, intellectuals—precisely as it always has

The things we say, the complaints we make against the world ^*comprise*^ the innermost nature of our culture, its most basic beliefs and its fundamental values. The teen age gangs who attack people in the streets with tire chains, and the older failures who gather in the John Birch society are those who are not able to play any of the roles which have been defined as meaningful by our culture, what they want ~~is to~~ ^*is a revolution which would*^ overthrow us who are pre-empting the meaningful roles, the lives which have meaning ~~within this culture~~ as meaning is defined by this culture.

It so happens that I   well,

happen to occupy a position at the precise apex of the pyramid: there is no one who outranks me. First, because I am a poet, ~~which is~~ which gives me a position somewhere in the upper layers of the cultural pyramid, and finally because I am an unknown poet, which places me ~~in~~ ^*at*^ the ~~highest position of our society~~. I outrank the President of the United States. It is understood that if the President had the temerity to invite me for dinner, I would contemptuously refuse. If I did not refuse, I would no longer be an unknown poet, of course, and would no longer outrank the President.[17]

those who have not ~~been granted~~ ^*achieved*^ a role defined as meaningful by this culture, and who lead, therefore, lives without meaning and without drama and without honor.

What they want, what they so violently and dangerously want, is a revolution which will overthrow us who are pre-empting the meaningful roles in this society.

(ADDED IN 1969: Would they want a redefinition of meaningful roles))[18]

+ + +

we become preoccupied in discussing what people should do—probably the habit of our political conceptions, and forget the actual fact which is simply that people find themselves born—and in unimaginable numbers—without preparation and quite involuntarily and must try to find something to do with the fact, some want at least not to find it pure suffering.

Finding them alive, we take the fact for granted, and prescribe their duties. They do not.

THAT WOMEN HAVE NO HISTORY——the women thought at any time just as now—*we speak of the thought of the 17th Century vs. today—*
We do not mean the women. They felt then as they do now.

The tendency of women to think medically, to judge ideas according as they seem healthy or not, according as they lead toward life and the proliferation of life—. The long period of an optimistic materialism, an anthropocentric rationalism, found men and women very much in agreement. Its breakdown renders communication almost impossible between men and women—

i.e.—simply stated: When men are not committed to the support and proliferation of life, they cannot get along with women.

Tho it may be equally true that those women not committed to the burgeoning of life have little use for men—. The ecology has only that purpose—

The self finds itself involuntarily alone and defined, and is filled with bitter anger, and greed

the miracle is—[19]

We must cease to believe
In secret names and unexpected phrases
Which will burst the world—

Sweden, however—.   But it works out again and again to the same conclusion—. The woman is swept up, carried away. It is the man who must do the sweeping up, the carrying away, still himself, still only his own force under an open sky.

+ + +

Nor—an intermittent history? Or even that their history must be recounted independently, an independent history. As the history of the nineteenth century is a history of the forming of nations, of the accumulation of capital, the elaboration of the machine and the organization of labor. But the history of women in the nineteenth century is characterized by Florence Nightingale and Carrie Nation—?

Do women have a history? or are they unchanged

And more beautiful

"The Virgin Mary"
Bronk's insistence on the capitals—The Virgin Mary would probably mean, of the virginism that one named mary. The title means, Mary, who is the Virgin. An indecipherable meaning.

A totally objective art, an art of caprice which means to say nothing of oneself or one's situation, an art of pure construction—

No artist think [illegible]tly of beauty or seeks directly for
the beauitiful [illegible] e works. He thinks ~~perhaps~~ of
illumination, of disclosure. He is concerned with emection,
but ~~only~~ of emotion which [illegible] Discloses
The blind emotion, blind sensation of background music,
of soft lightes which ~~many peop[le] mean when~~ they say
'beautiful' has nothing to do with th artists work.

what concerns the artist is that the thing
exists ---- and he starts with a ruined labguage, ~~the~~ [illegible]
abive language. The trouble is that it is possible to

Must try to get back to what does exist theonta
to language which can confront, can stand.

which is not merely a seriois of self indulgent
gestures, indications of attitude or sentiment.

a poem may be devoted to giving clear meaning to one
word.

Daybook II:II

Part 2 of the first "Pipe-Stem Daybook." Excisions include poem drafts, letters, and illegible writings.

+ + +

We will finally say God or we will be unable to say anything" *G.O.*

> *"What we know must be known to its roots, for we shall never know anything until we know its causes." Meister Eckhart, Sermons, 16*[1]

+ + +

The theology which decrees that God is love is intelligent theology. If there is a theology in the universe, there is will, desire—Eros, the will, *the erotic*

in the circumstance of being alive

I should think they would be aware of a fault not only in their reasoning but in their motivation. That see God only as "the guarantor of human greatness"; ^*or the guarantor of a real ethic*^ they are thinking therefore of humanity, not of god. can conceive of god? Maybe negatively. The first negotiation would be the rejection of that word and of all words, both the pronoun
he and the noun god.

Eros—the will—cannot act for itself

+++

The alternative to the erotic is the ~~INERT~~ INANIMATE

+++

One must remember that man is said to have evolved not, to begin with, from the amoebae, but from hydrogen gas. There is no teleology recognized in that process; that is, if at any stage in the evolution there has been anything in the universe which desired to further the process, that desire was irrelevant. The thing took place entirely by chance. ~~Time~~ It is said that the process occupied a great many years. The only question is—Does one believe it?

Eros—the will—drifts in the ontological

I have been in the habit of doing things my own way. And I have been willing to pay for it. I realize, tho, that it has been pure good fortune that I have been able to ~~pay for~~ ^*afford*^ it[2]

Cold water flats—but i think that of all those who committ'd suicide in the 16 century, none killed themselves because there was no such thing as hot running water in the world.

Diction. the distinction is in the words I do not use, more than in the words I do use. I use the words for large and for small often. Because scale is important, just because it is subjective.

+ + +

I work sometimes for eight hours or so, fiddling with corrections. But sometimes I am so tired in two or three hours of effort that I'm shaken. Possible an element of self dramatization. But it is also fear. I ~~realize that~~ nothing so extraordinary appears in the poems, ~~Besides~~ and once the thing has been written there is no need to find it overwhelming. But for me the sense of thinking beyond what I already know ~~which~~ ^*or what someone already knows*^ is terrifying. It would not be terrifying in abstract terms. It is terrifying in terms of the objects around me, ~~of the things I have seen or will see~~

+ + +

No artist think[s direc]tly of beauty or seeks directly for
the beautiful [ ] ^*but*^ thinks ~~perhaps~~ of illumination, of disclosure.
He is concerned with emotion, but of emotion which ~~Discloses~~
Discloses The blind emotion, blind sensation of background music, of soft lights which ~~many people mean when~~ ^[ ]^ ~~they say~~ "beautiful" has nothing to do with the artists work.[3]

what concerns the artist is that the thing exists——and he starts with a ruined language ^~~He must~~ *day by day and then by man, destroyed*^ achieves language. The trouble is that it is possible to

Must try to get back to what does exist the onta
to language which can confront, can stand.

which is not merely a series of self-indulgent gestures, indications of attitude or sentiment.

a poem may be devoted to giving clear meaning to one word.

Wi

What he says is irrevocable and his word determines what shall be

~~[illegible]~~

Whatever comes out of his mouth cannot be changed and his word determines the days to come.

[illegible]

I think ~~the question~~ asked more frankly, ~~would be:~~ ~~is~~ it more imprtant to produce art or to ~~en[illegible]~~ in politics [illegible]. Of course I cannot pretend to asnwer such a question. I co ld point this out, however, that art and pltitcal action ~~are in~~ precise opposition in this regard: that ~~[illegible]~~ it can always be quite easitly shown that political action is going to be valuable; it is difficult ever to prove ~~that it has been in the past~~ [illegible]. Whereas art is precisely in the opposite case; it seems always impossible to prove that it is going to be valuable, and yet it is always quite clear that ~~in the past it has been.~~ [illegible]

I think one deos what he is m st moved to do.
However I could point to an interesting contrast: it can alwys be shown etc

[illegible]

Daybook II:III

Part 3 of the first "Pipe-Stem Daybook." Excisions include poem drafts, ephemera, and illegible writings.

+ + +

translation;

A business letter commonly employs the current usage whose meaning is evident only thru its occurrence. "Yours of the 15th inst." I agree had better be translated into whatever phrase is current in another country; it is a matter of translating into another's mores, not merely into another language. But a poet who is worth translating, tho he may have employed conventional idioms of his language, is also aware of what he is saying, and has in fact given the matter some thought——— aware of what the words say—and must be translated as literally as possible. An excellent example is Norton's translation of Rilke "I wish I had someone to read to / By someone to sit and be." The problem was not to make German into English, but to make English into German.[1]

+ + +

Since human intelligence has thus inevitably failed in its task, one can only hope that for the immediate future things will somehow settle themselves, thanks to the natural resources of human mediocrity, in other words, thanks to a kind of animal shrewdness adjusting itself to the natural pressures of history. But taking as a whole the phase of the world's history which we have reached, it has become a commonplace remark to say that we have crossed the threshold of the Apocalypse.

Maritain[2]

There is developing in man a longing for nothingness, a desire not to be.

The "confessional" poetry—. Not always sensationalism. It expresses—in the most honest and the most radical way—the major fact of this century, that we have lost the faith in man which was the foundation of 19th century rationalism

"anthropomorphic rationalism" A rationalism which derived its force and its purpose from the idea of the infinite possibilities of man

That man is "good" —that man is gregarious, I suppose, and must act, at least some of the time, accordingly. According to ^*In keeping with*^ the interests of a gregarious animal. The general realization that "we live because we breathe"

When we weary of the expression of despair? What art?

Heidegger: he finds the recognition of Being in the experience of Nothingness, somewhat as Camus finds it in the experience of despair.

Insofar as idealism centers around the human mind, it becomes a dream or a nightmare . . . It is not true of Leibnitz nor of Plotinus—. Perhaps they should be called Vitalists, for this is reason, rather than Idealist? No *doubt. Certainly they mean to describe an objective universe.*

And the pure joy / of the mineral fact[3]

"IS" definite as primary intellectual ~~assertion~~ intuition

+ + +

It is not true that the Christian religion has been a religion of slaves. It has been a religion of emperors and empires. The doctrine of evil, the struggle between good and evil, the doctrine of the devil, ~~has been necessary to it~~: from that doctrine derives the possibility ^*that man could ever enlist*^ ~~of the enlistment of man~~ on the side of God. ^*Thus*^ true monotheism tends ^*of course it does*^ to disregard political and social concerns.

I think it probable that man cannot long exist without faith—I think it possible that man will not exist forever.

Offensive rhetoric—in that it is all so much easier for the writer than for the man on the cross

We really have no hope of faith, and hardly a hope of doubt. *Therefore, hardly hope.*[4]

+ + +

The weakness of Imagism—a man writes of the moon rising over a pier who knows nothing about piers and is disregarding all that he knows about the moon.

Possible indeed that human life cannot long exist without faith—it is probable that human life will not exist forever.

Such writers whose philosophizing at every step means "to discover the most advantageous intellectual position and to connive with the times"——to discover and "philosophically" justify those opinions which seem proper.[5] But philosophy, like art, must be free—the actual sight ^*indication*^ of truth at the course of each word.

To say again of the factories—the massive heart
Of the present, the presence

In the factories the young workman
Elated among the men

+ + +

There is not a "cure" for us, a reversal of some wrong or perverse decision which we have made somewhere or sometime. It is the death of time which has passed, the accumulation of knowledge which has confronted us with despair.

We simply know too much

+ + +

Marianne Moore—
The elaborate form of the verse is not, of course, the promiscuousness of decoration, but chastity, the involutions of chastity. It is a social aesthetic, one of the rare triumphs of gentility. I cannot believe that the achievement has relevance for many people today, ~~that it solves anything for us~~, that it answers any question which we have ever asked ourselves, but it is a statement which has indeed required the care and art which she has brought to it.[6]

It is in the end a machine of pride, another machine of pride and of avoidance, which has no value for us.

A machine which is able to reconcile even ^*the*^ jerboa and other ^*small*^ desert animals to the formal conversation of the drawing room:

fastidiousness

An ethic of fastidiousness

+ + +

"belief" actually means in revelation. Otherwise a word that means "that which we can know nothing about" is a word without meaning. *"That of which we cannot speak, of that we must remain silent"*[7]

For "chastity of diction" write "decency of diction," the phrase being more chaste

The Strong Man

Which is lower class
Of him—to be so—
And moreover girls dont much want him.
His young wife is far too womanly,
They will get nowhere.
He is probably a truck driver
Or a crane operator.

The women vying with the glassy savagery of the cities

The mammal horde

Looking up the companionway
From the cabin, ^*and*^ on deck
The ^*strong*^ rail shining
Silently in the sun.

A sterile excitement—as jazz.
at least arbitrary excitement

The mystery of truth!

+ + +

A man loses a dear friend by his accidentally falling from a plane. The man spends the time during which his friend is falling pleasantly enough, perhaps in reading, and breaks abruptly into lamentation only after his friend has hit the ground.

+ + +

Well, I am interested in a conversation. With those who are companions. But I am not interested in wowing the public, much less in mystifying it. Nor in entertaining it either. Why should I wish to do that?

The parakeet's heart—
Which must be microscopic—
Is filled with a most impertinent
Love, a masterful
Affection—

To see if one can see in the open—

In the open of the common rubble

One is grateful for existence——the "love of God as Creator"—
One wants VERY much to exist

The tide running fast in the narrow channel—the calm of all sources

        The Loves of Children
It is because the child given time
And sanctuary—world enough
And time[8]
Has not yet made so many choices as to have no choice left.
Therefore one sees the human, the—

To drive roots
Deep enough into sand, gravel,
Rock, rubble, the common rubble—

For their lives

Those who read nothing live,
It seems to me,
Live in too short a span of time

In the machine of greed and pride
Which is about what they hear
In the populace areas.

To find———   for anyone!

That time in the soddy gorge
Thru which the river (the Caves in the Dordonne)

The Zulu girl[9]

+ + +

The women vying with the glassy savagery of the cities—

A part of the attack on this society is the destructive mores of precisely this society. And at one with it in the desire for a New Model each February—

Philistine, after protest, welcomes the new toy

and the greater part of that attack an attack not on society but on art, on the obstinacy of art
art which defines ^ *establishes* ^ a relationship

My language which proves I am not alone.

Obstinate

Marisol: they walk in off the street, and are confronted with themselves—.[10] The satire may not be ~~justified~~ *social:* she seems perhaps to be accusing them of existing, but that is another question. There is no question of the effectiveness of the art. It replaces the self-glorification and self-deception of the New York School, which was indeed absurd and moribund, one would have thought, from the beginning.[11]

For chastity of diction write
"decency of diction"
Because this is more decent

+ + +

Does philosophy burden itself unnecessarily with the terms "mind" and "subject"? Is it not possible simply to hold that the world contains, among other things, living organisms? The problem of knowledge would therefore reduce to psychological or physiological problems. It would result, I would suppose, in a pragmatist solution, since it is clear that the reason cannot judge its own reasonableness except by its results in action. And actual analysis of the formation of the canon of "the reasonable," both of reasonable processes and reasonable assumptions, might show that it has been formed and selected by such texts.

I DO NOT MEAN TO PRESCRIBE ~~AN OPINION OR~~ AN IDEA,
BUT TO RECORD THE EXPERIENCE OF THINKING IT

Schwerner's poem—which takes ~~my work~~ in its major sense;
the reference to Akiba who looked at the underworld and remained sane.[12]

The tremendous power of sanity.

MINIMAL ART—They like art because they believe it is less important than anything else, its meaning the most contained, the most self-contained, its emotion the most ephemeral.

+ + +

What he says is irrevocable and his word determines what shall be

Whatever comes out of his mouth cannot be changed and his word determines the days to come

Not really a question. I think that as a question and asked as a philosophical question I think it would be this: is

I think the question asked more frankly would be: is it more important to produce art or to ~~engage in~~ ^*take political action*^. Of course I cannot pretend to answer such a question. I could point this out, however, that art and political action are in precise opposition in this regard: that it can always be quite easily shown that political action is going to be valuable; it is difficult to ever prove ~~that it has been in the past~~ ^*that political action has been valuable*^. Whereas art is precisely the opposite case; it seems always impossible to prove that it is going to be valuable, and yet it is always quite clear that ~~in the past it has been.~~ ^*the art of the past has been of value to humanity. I offer it only as a suggestion that art lacks in political action, not action. One does what he is most moved to do.*^

I think one does what he is most moved to do.

However I could point to an interesting contrast: it can always be shown etc.

+ + +

The automobile is a symbol of money—Not the other way round. The gamblers: they are dealing with the very heart of the thing, with money, like a heart or a brain operation

+ + +

William's mother remembers only youth and childhood——
Because everything was open, because there seemed not limitation of the possibilities, because———a "natural religion"?
The routine things later, the biologic things, the ontological things later forgotten, meaningless, a failure or disappointment. Linda now restoring to herself the expectations of childhood, re-gathering them

Range of reason age 99
but—those "who pass thru the tragedy of their times"
not without flinching, and not without recognizing the absolute tragedy ~~of the non-existence of God~~

I know that people have only their lives,
and many their lives disregard

it is born
in the ontology
Eros—the
word—
Eros

William's thought of the West Indies of his mother's time—[13]
The ladies and gentlemen drove carriages in the little villages, the vendors were vendors, the slaves were slaves—a people not emerged into history, living in the midst of a number of cultures.

a people not conscious of themselves or conscious of themselves primarily as descendents, a people without ontological responsibility, acceptant—

+ + +

Such force

Had moved us—

maine: to exist with people

airplane: in the air
Lit by the moon

If we are alone; language. what would we make of
sexuality, sexual difference?

fool, look out the window
And write[14]

My father's letter about the Depression—and breakfast in bed. That Depression almost cost us our reason; we could not bear the sight of what had happened. It threw us into twenty years of political frenzy.[15]

Pamela Hanford Johnson, in review of Wallace Fowlies's A Reading of Proust in ny times book review, July 19, 1964[16]
"Do you remember the labyrinth in the children's puzzle book, a typographical maze, with a score of entrances, only one of which leads to

the core? Prousts "A la Recherche du Temps Perdue" is, in design, not unlike it, except that all entrances lead to the core.

the poem: all entrances lead to the core—

"Any one writes poems"

I try to understand—or perhaps I try to understand certain things—and I try not to be alone.

That little business
of the nerves // Is stopped in him—and this is no longer/
Our brother

+ + +

the one poem of Schwerner's;

I would think it should be omitted. Fucking and even bucking—~~Alright~~ ^*Ok by me*^. Basic activities. But mucking? Unless I merely don't follow the poem. As I indeed I don't. ~~I have no idea what it means to 'say'. But I dislike the form and the tone of the poem.~~[17] Certainly words can be reduced to nothing, but it is hardly OUR job! Someone will do it sooner or later; that it is not ~~in fact the going thing~~ is due only to the fortunate fact that the gambler's money has not been thrown into poetry as it has been thrown into painting. But to produce such work is merely to be patronized—in the modern import of the word—by the patronizing rich. At most. The ^*playful*^ rich ~~who like to play a little~~. Between deals, and in view of the income tax structure. A ~~rather~~ weary ^*cruel*^ *annoying game,* in more primitive times, *it consisted*

in more early American times it consisted of lighting cigars with ten dollar bills.

BOYS ROOM—almost a cliche; the artist remains a child. But the artists room is indeed a boys room. Incapable of being deceived by riding a rolls royce. Or once deceived, ceases to be an artist. It is—paradoxically—a sense of reality and [name of person]; will be a person. Which is all any of us can be. With a special color, atmosphere, a person, a new person, herself,

^*and the conviction that there is something or other which would be a clear victory over something or other*^ "That little boy?!" the girl needing to be taken into the adult world, needing a man who will take her into the adult world. And even convince her. But who will want to know her when she arrives there?
All this is obvious, and beyond this—

sexually exciting tho, probably. even the unbeautiful banker, a real man, panting for breath; a "real" man—not a boy—.[18]

Eugenics— *The Strong Man*

It is lower class
And moreover girls dont much want him.
~~*His wife is small and womanly*~~
His young wife is far too womanly,
They will get nowhere.
He is probably a truck driver
Or a crane operator.

+ + +

For the atheist or the agnostic it is terrible to die—One cannot reconcile himself to it. It would be still more terrible to live forever.[19]

School: I set myself to live through it. And did. (I think I did)

I mean I too dislike poetry -- in fact I dislike art -- except as a last resort.

or, it need not sound quite so philistine. If I can easily think more profoundly outside the poem than in it, I xxxxxxxxx find the verse irritating.

The images; small narratives within the poem

— Stone, stone, we are dust to each other while we exist —

Protestantism -- merely the currently acceptable ideas given a religious tone in order to achieve unanimity -- Neither a comsology nor a methaphysic; possibly a social contract.

The big dent (Dump) from (form) of the moon

We awake in the same moment -- etc, means that one could understand himself only in relation to the universe.

June, who I begin to realize has genius, who is very, very extreme --. She does not like most people, take comfort in the idea of continuity, of children and of people who knew her. She hates and resents those who will replace her. She dreams of living, of herself, by herself, forever. The elevator poems, which I misunderstood ---- They meant, if she could do everything herself, if she were not dependent on these technicians who insisted they could not take the car further, she might be able to emerge into ---------- might rise above everything. And independent of everything.

It is surely an attempt to conquer the universe — —

If june should write her metaphysic, it would be this:

Life sets me a problem; which I must solve. Just that probelem, and just as it is set. If I solve it, if I conquer, I willnot die' Not then, not in victory. I will be set another problem; another life --

yet her faith is not perfect. She feels -- But if I fail? And in defeat -- defeated like others, dfeated like nobodies -- she would want to be comforted, cared ofr -- not to be alone. But that above is her mtaphysic; and it is not ordinary -- it has nothing whatever to do with current 'nicenesses', with current humanism --

Perhaps it is the metaphysic of great men —

Daybook II:IV

Part 4 of the first "Pipe-Stem Daybook." Excisions include poem drafts, drafts of letters, ephemera, and illegible writings.

+ + +

I suppose I mean that I must admit a great deal to myself ^*in order to have written books*^. And that a great many things may disappear. *(*Perhaps hope, perhaps meaning. And if it does, would it not be more reasonable not to write, or at least not to print the book?*)* But I cannot say to myself I will write if——That is just to guarantee meretriciousness. *So, a book of just understanding it. And perhaps that is what I will do.*[1]

"totally free from nothingness"[2] ^*and death*^ (Without nothingness) A statement I accept. But I don't think the phrase can be freed of negatives.

An age "of anthropocentric optimism has ended in human devastation"[3]

Since one does not in any case live forever, and since the furthest possible extremes of age may not be desirable to experience, it is entirely reasonable to risk one's life for a purpose, far more reasonable than people say. But since one can give his life only once, it is true that he must be guided simply by his feelings, by what happens to matter to him—

If we are to understand anything—and I do not believe we are to understand anything, to understand absolute truth or to know anything which is relevant to absolute truth, but if we are surely we must start at the beginning. And surely not with a bloody and murderous institution, which has been the bloodiest institution on the face of the earth

Returning from the country:
"It is all still out there"

+ + +

It seems likely that every publisher

and apparently will not print me at all. Which seems to be a fact, a fact which probably indicates something about France and England. Russia also would not print me, and so far as I know I have no Esquimeaux followers. Apparently, Bushmen and Esquimeaux, and no doubt large numbers of Americans, find significance in different things than I do.

Self-sufficiency and moral purpose are unreconcilable

Ethel: her addressing an audience and not addressing herself. Which is to say, not *thinking*.[4]

The serious artist: that he addresses only his equals; that he means to say what only he can say.

Leni: who are "people"? Only people one doesn't know?[5]

Art as old as civilization. If one can add one thing to so long a history, one color or shape or tone, one perception to so long a history, that is a great deal to do. If he tries to do a great many things he will probably be repeating what has been done better.

The sunset; madness
to deny
Our involvement
In ~~all this~~ ^*all events,*^ and insanity
To believe it

Narrative—The climax of the poem is the judging of the word "Permanance": which by then has another meaning. (Synonym of "eternal" of course. It is the point of the poem that one can't intuit much the meaning without the intuition of the word "eternal"[6]

+ + +

James Baldwin describing the misery of his childhood:
"it was books that taught me that the things that tormented me most were the things that connected me with all the people who were alive, or who had ever been alive."—And, I think, might have added: it was that knowledge which saved ~~my~~ ^*his*^ life.[7]

I wrote—to Billy?—that I thought all a poem could do for people was to say "me too"[8]

I think there has been a very long experiment in atheism. And that it has proven insupportable. Whether or not it is true. (I take the majority of church members to be atheist. Their membership in the church hides from them not so much their atheism, as the possibility of a religion.)

Russia—Well, but the Russians have not had a very long experiment in atheism. And during its course they have been very carefully kept to a limited number of ideas. There is simply a great deal they have not yet become aware of that a large part of the world IS aware of——. And none of which is answered by dialectical materialism.

+ + +

"The Negro Rights movement and the forces of public order are moving on collision courses."[9] And the established Negro leadership is losing control of the movement. Of which the result could only be a successful Negro revolution, which seems obviously impossible, or a pacification by force of the Negro people. Which last would result in a gradual and perhaps fairly far-reaching program of amelioration of the situation of the Negros, but would bring them into an improved economic situation as a policed minority.

It is probable that the Negroes could not have avoided the situation—. The Southerners had defied federal law, and the government had been afraid, and probably unable to enforce law. The Negro militants could not have continued forever to find volunteers for jail sentences, for beatings and murders: school children, northern students and southern students, adults—Surely at least they could not have continued into another generation to have called for heroism of that kind and degree. If the Southerners could merely defy the law, purely legal methods became useless; there arose a situation in which perhaps nothing could be done except by Negro defiance of the law.

It is not a question of revolution, since there can be no question of a "take over" by a ten percent minority. But the situation resembles the situation of revolution: the prospect of the oppressed—and therefore brutalized, or even if not brutalized, those with little or no stake in the present order—momentarily destroying, here and there, the public order and the security of life.

If one "did something"? If one joined again in some way? The suppression of the Negroes is clearly neither a permanent nor a tolerable solution, even if it is possible. But I certainly do not welcome riot. And least of all a riot in which I am not free to choose sides. The attitude of the reformist, then. The attempt to get concessions before violence breaks loose, to help, if one can help, the established leadership to obtain victories. What other attitude? But one can comfort himself at least by honesty, and by acting in clear self-interest, as the Negroes act also—as they should, and in such ways as they are forced to act—in clear self-interest.[10]

+ + +

At some time in the future, the Negro people will have the right to vote—and will be voting Democrat, Republican, Birchite, prohibitionist, etc—and equality of employment, etc . . . And the nationalist speeches and essays will sound like the stupidest of American Jingoism written during the Mexican American war.

(with the universe:)

to deny our kinship is madness
to accept it is insanity

Louis: Does not lack the quality of intelligence but the quality of honesty

The lack of ~~poetry~~ literature in England—is simply that England does not have a New Directions nor any press?

Its impossible to be as clever
as he wants to be—   even if he <u>were</u>
measured by clever
-ness[11]

+ + +

I was not on the March to Washington. I have not been in any sit-ins, and I have not been in any Southern jails, and am not in a position to lecture anyone about support of the Negro movement ^*or civil rights*^. Except to say that I think discrimination disgraceful, inexcusable, and criminal.

But since I have an immediate and personal interest in an attitude that ~~identifies~~ ^*regards*^ itself as militant among a growing number of intellectuals—including Leroi Jones, a nice fellow and an excellent writer—who however does not hesitate in his militance to write crushingly in the pages of Kulchur about "Jewish millionaires," ^*I would*^ gladly lecture on that.

^*It seems to me probable that a*^ decision by a Negro intellectual to take up a Black Muslim position is, in practice, a decision merely not to participate in Marches or voters' registration drives in the South, and might therefore not be worth discussing. But if it has any influence on Negro attitudes, I doubt if it is one which anyone—anyone at all—has reason to welcome. Unless as a diversion in intellectual discussion. Or in the theatre.

But I am tired of anti-bourgeois manifestos by people who dont know what the word means or have deliberately forgotten. Bourgeois—the city man, the merchant and the manufacturer, the beneficiary of "free enterprise." If they are anti-bourgeois, they want to terminate industrial production, or socialize production, or? or? They must mean something. Or they mean simply that they want to go their own way. Well, so do I. And I intend to do it. But that inconveniences the bourgeois very little, so far as I know.

Leroi— he has a moderate talent of invective. And simply has been fortunate to have proved a case for it.[12]

+ + +

Of course the non-violent leaders represent a tiny minority, a minority of the bourgeoisie minority. And of course such people as Malcolm X are essentially more popular leaders. And when the basic masses of the Negro people begin to move we will discover how fascist-minded a population—both Negro and white—this country contains. "When I hear the word culture I reach for my pistol"—a very popular slogan. More popular in this country than in any country of the world.

Of course, SNCC and such organizations have fought not only for justice for Negro people, but also for ~~some meaning~~ ^*a content*^ in the movement beyond the correction of ~~that~~ injustice, for some content which would be a part of an effort to move the country. Many are facing life sentences for their part in it. And the Negro people dont like to talk about them at all. There were at least three hundred thousand whites on the March to Washington and Negro people dont care to talk about that either. ~~Who~~ ^*What American*^ would? it is talking about principaled action. When the chronically unemployed move into action they will demand jobs at the expense of "foreigners"—because who else? And they will demand in the professions the exclusion of Jews—because who else? And they will having nothing to do with any peace movement which might so easily cost colonies and jobs. There has never been an uprising so devoid of actual programs other than pure and simple economic self-interest ^*within the machinery of free enterprise*^, a desire to share in the spoils. There has never been a popular movement so devoid of ideas, and now arises the demand for fewer ideas, for less idealism, for nothing more than the right to compete on equal terms with all the disadvantaged. And they will compete, they will fight—<u>against</u> the disadvantaged. And they will <u>fight</u>. And if they fight for legislation ^*and legal protection*^ they will fight on the streets. And if they fight in the streets, because a minority cant fight the armed forces of the country, they will fight their neighbors. And next door to them of course—the foreigners. And the Jews. And the Commies. And the conscientious objectors. And all those who have not attended the simplest of self interest or the simplest search for another bottle of beer. Some children beaten in Williamsburg. A lot of people beaten in a lot of places. That is to say, in a lot of slum districts. If that's the revolution—. High times a-cummin. Happy days! But what will the "militance" be that attacks Jews and foreigners and children and elderly men in the slums and the public parks? What can it be but American corruption and self-hatred: hatred of the poor and the oppressed. Uncle Tomism raised to viciousness, sycophancy and cowardice and brutality? Surely nothing <u>more</u> than that.[13]

+ + +

the hazard of social work—that it is a principled work and therefore one must take it seriously. But day by day it discusses only the most primitive, the most simple questions: budgets, the buying of groceries, getting into a hospital or home from a hospital, housework—^*and organizational problems*^. That is, the ^*simplest*^ possible level of thought. ^*simple is definitely American*^ If they were thinking only of such matters for their own benefit, they would be aware that they were minimal concerns. Because they are thinking "for others" they become unaware that it is ~~primitive thinking~~ ^*inadequate thought.*^

It is these two facts together which render it deadly to the social worker. They are people who enter the work because they are principled. And they are quickly trained to devote all of their thinking to such matters as the price of vegetables and the quality of the plumbing. ^*which is inadequate thinking*^ And to think of these things only in the most helpless and remote way, to think of them as shoppers. Not as people who could get running water into houses if they lived three feet from the Mississippi River.

+ + +

Nevertheless, the pop art is not a caprice. It was inevitable. Fifty years of Wasteland—surrealism, Hopper, Wyeth, Eliot's early work—. But the surrealists were elaborate, Hopper and Wyeth are almost sentimental or can be seen as purely sentimental, and one sees Eliot's rhetoric, the beauty of the rhetoric, more clearly than one sees the wasteland. But pop art simply presents it, the waste land itself, unmistakable and irresistibly and undeniably. Of course it depends for its meaning on the art gallery, and on the ability of the art gallery to retain its meaning. An ash can on the East Side is the artist's subject matter; an ash can in a gallery is his expression.

Like a bull in a china shop: it is striking for a while. After that, the china shop becomes a bull pen, and the bull is an ordinary bull.

+ + +

Final question, last preoccupation, there is nothing beyond it

Seems ^*to me*^ to mean that all truth is empirical. Which is simply Aquinas' Veritas sequitour esse rerum.[14] A statement which seems to me, by a kind of poetic process, a process of remembering one's own experience, inescapable. As I recall it, I found the thing. The world could have been different in any respect. Including "circles."

This country belongs to the Gods

I can see nothing at all except that one encounters the thing. And, it is impossible not to say, encounters himself. For which also the conditions were all present, were all "given." And encounters in himself the passion of logic which, like the young man's desire to sleep with Debbie Reynolds, is unlikely to be satisfied, but can lead to crime, to crimes of violence.

I really can't see how any truth is not empirical, or ~~that one can do any thing but reapeat~~ that it is encountered. Or that one can do more than repeat the encounter

> *(The limited whole*
> *which it is not—)*

+ + +

What created us—"our father"—is the
constituents of the universe. What creates form———

The smile on the face of

Blake's Tyger[15]

The self-willed entity which is absolutely single & single & un-caused. It is necessary for us to conceive that there is such a term. It is almost impossible to suffer if there is not.

+ + +

On Leibnitz

If a man is propelled by rocket to a point near the moon, the concept will form irresistibly in his mind of a huge curved surface hanging in space before him. ~~Had he not been objectively moved The mind may form concepts "of itself"—certainly thru the internal senses—but tho one may form vivid concepts, he could not have forced a concept to form in his mind of such vividness—~~

he could not have formed that concept ~~of such vividness~~ so vividly if he had stayed home.

The internal senses:

without external senses, the mind would form in concepts of time. Because the mind thinks consecutively, and therefore ~~creates~~ The mind thinking itself, forms the concept of time.

But—

If the world is matter
It is impenetrable[16]

+ + +

Young people—even the brilliant young people—tend to address their immediate elders, whether in hatred or in love. A long step from there to the dialogue carried out across a number of centuries which is literature.

+ + +

it is certainly not difficult now to ~~accept that~~ ^*believe that*^ the ideas of space and time are indeed ideas, and that if one's senses were different one would experience reality differently. It seems that the distinction between atomic particles and atomic force could be expressed in the same way. It is surely not a sufficiently powerful idea on which to base the immortality of the soul—

In the primitive act of consciousness
There are the internal senses

The basic constituents of the Universe, which can only be encountered—

It is hardly the image of a familiar idea, a familiar concept ~~*—I am conscious of trying to say it— That is, I am conscious of trying to achieve a form—*~~
I am conscious of trying to make a statement. That is, I am of trying to achieve a form

+ + +

We talk to young people—even give advice to young people—"in the arts." It is a peculiar game, of course;   Tho I had regarded myself as

a poet—O, at the age of ten or twelve—I had thought it dangerous if not fatal, I had always assumed that to write verse was to condemn oneself to public insult. I had certainly never imagined that one might further himself socially or financially by art— I took thirty years between books—
I had at no time considered writing within an established art-world.

The fact is, we are hopelessly caught in phenomena.
The mind's inherent sense of logic is a phenomenon.

"the senses have their own nature, and therefore
cannot disclose absolute truth—

"The mind has ~~an inherent logic~~ ^its own nature^, and therefore
supplies necessary truth" a double standard.

often we feel our hand forced by it.
against "our wills"
Shut the mind—like shutting the eyes—

+ + +

Not a temporal question, but a question of cause. An electrical field exists because a magnet is present. We may say that the magnet creates the electrical field. But if the magnet was always present, the electrical field was always present—

When we hear a train—we understand that the train is not identical with the sound waves that reach us. But we understand also that there is a train there.

We say that we hear the train, but know that we "hear" the sound or the "sound waves." In the same way, the train need not really be what we feel or see, tho the sight or the sensation is caused by the actuality of the train.

There is a quotation on the fly leaf of the book which admits that I knew that you would not care for it. I do not mean to dismiss you. I regret that you ~~will~~ ^*would*^ not like it, I would be pleased if you did like it. I had to make a choice. Or rather, I had to make that choice. There are a thousand miles—I would say, of mist—between us. That we can hear each other at all is the extraordinary power of language.[17]

Leni, the poems about Mary and Linda and my friends and myself.[18] What do you mean by "people"? People I don't know?

Ourselves at 20—We meant to entangle ourselves at the roots of the world. We were certainly not thinking of "success," nor of social sophistications.[19]

Someone hits me—in the dark—with an axe—for no reason that I know. See what has been done to me!

"The undeniability / of the real"—Leibnitz[20]

of everything which is real
–G.O.

If the world is matter, it is ~~un~~ impenetrable absolutely. The recognition of impenetrability houses the hope of intelligibility.[21]

+ + +

I felt for many years as D. feels.[22] And we devoted ourselves to creating happiness for the three of us, and for a few friends and their children so far as possible. I could not have continued as I was going with my early poems—there was too much time ahead of us. But now what will happen to us in twenty years is——. We must discuss it again, we must try to understand it.

+ + +

Games—One sits down to a game, and emerges, when it is finished, into the same world one sat down in, having passed some time

And

An old man
In rags
Crying
For his own death

+ + +

The bonds between things that are—.
Therefore stood in my dark house.
Why does one agonize
Over it?   "Truth without passion,

Passion without truth," games
And enterprises

And necessity, which keeps us sane;

The search for truth   is a passion, not a necessity

+ + +

In the rain, the smoke from the chimneys
Flies in little lumps of smoke
Going fast in the wind over the roofs

Puddles no less than rivers
Bricks no less than Alps, it is for them one lives—

he walked down the hallways and past doors
And he came necessarily to a door
Thru which he passed
walked

writing a poem—I think of what happened, what I saw, what I felt ^*what I believed*^—. I test the words and the cadences and the form for clarity—clarity, I mean, as against pure mud. That is all I think about.

The final look of things.

The poem (narrative) depends for its "argument" on vividness—One might regard it as incoherent in the way that a man may seem incoherent whose argument consists finally in repeating—"But look, But look—!"

incoherent in the manner of a man who repeats "but look, but look"—coherent and convincing enuf to those who will or can look—

+ + +

I mean I too dislike poetry[23] (—in fact I dislike art—
except as a last resort.

or, it need not sound quite
so philistine.

If I can easily think more profoundly outside the poem than in it, I find the verse irritating.

The images;   small narratives within the poem

Stone, stone, we are tied to each other
while we exist

Protestantism—merely the currently acceptable ideas given a religious tone in order to achieve unanimity—neither a cosmology nor a metaphysic; possibly a social contract.

---

the big dumb form of the moon

We awake in the same moment—etc. means
that one could understand himself only in
relation to the universe.[24]

June, who I begin to realize has *genius,* who is very, very extreme—. She does not, like most people, take comfort in the idea of continuity, of children and of people who know her. She hates and resents those who will replace her. She dreams of living, of herself, by herself, forever. The elevator poems, which I misunderstood—— They meant if she could do everything herself, if she were not dependant on these technicians who insist they could not take the car further, she might be able to emerge into——— might rise above everything. And independent of everything

it is simply an attempt to deny her the universe—

If June should write ~~a~~ ^*her*^ metaphysic, it would be this:[25]
Life sets me a problem; which I must solve. Just that problem, and just as it is set. If I solve it, ~~I will~~ if I conquer, I will not die. Not then, not in victory. I will be set another problem; another life—

yet her faith is not perfect. She feels—But if I fail? And in defeat—defeated like others, defeated like nobodies—she would want to be comforted, cared for—not to be alone. But that above is her metaphysic; and it is not ordinary— it has nothing whatever to do with current "nicenesses," with current humanism—

Perhaps it is the metaphysic of great men—

+ + +

Humanism cannot persist simply as love for the
victim It is easy to love the victim.

A materialist humanism depended on a social solution, the perfectibility of man. Or on a mystical humanism derived from existentialism; man the creator of reality. Which is too close to solipsism to sustain a consistent humanism—

Or perhaps a filial piety. We will be rewarded, we will be comforted, because we so want

I am talking of a bein

I am not ~~talking of~~ displaying a dialectic. I am talking of a vision. Only I am talking of any vision. of all vision

; but while I live I will speak, and while I have reason I must answer.

ll Esdras

The similarity is that he is pretty young -- one finds himself armed with some strength of character -- one may have felt it precisely ~~it~~ as one feels a sword at his side or to be flourished in the hand -- one come finally to think of even the armamnet of his own character as pure luck, a gift from god knows where --

When it becomes conviction it becomes poetic -- and nothing but conviction is poetry

'yoyr own things that grow up with you, you cannot undertsand

ll Esdaras

Nor does anything perish except that which can be transformed into soelthing else; that which has nothing into which it can be transformed does not perish Plotinus

Might -- like l -- translate Ou sont les neiges d'antoab as Who sent less needed aggs, Danton?

Danton?

NOT A DIALECTIC
BUT A VISION — Not a dialectic
But VISION

Daybook II:V

Part 5 of the first "Pipe-Stem Daybook." Excisions include poem drafts, drafts of letters, ephemera, and illegible writings.

+ + +

It is not certain now—nor is it moot—whether or not Oswald was the assassin of the president.

If Oswald was not the assassin, he must have been elaborately framed. And by the Dallas police.

Since the Dallas police permitted a "friend" of theirs, a man known to carry a gun, to approach Oswald in the police station, it is possible to believe that they deliberately connived at his murder. If indeed they did, what is to be made of the District Attorney's statement that the case of Oswald was closed by his murder, and would not be further investigated, nor further evidence given to the public.

Birmingham is not necessarily the only city in the south whose police chief is involved with racist groups. These groups have not made a secret of their fury against Kennedy.

This would be a picture of crisis, of violence which has got out of hand. It may well be an accurate picture of the state of affairs.

There is in everyone's mind—I suppose I mean the intellectuals—that something is going on, and perhaps we are fools. We begin to remember again how much the thing matters to us, how much we have at stake, how very endangered we are, how far we are from the belt-buckled semi-fascist population of the fanatic groups, and how very close we are to each other.

Seeing the news photos of Jacqueline Kennedy with her children, one realizes again what a very beautiful young woman she is, and recognizes her strength and her honor. The children stand quietly, and one remembers that such children understand speech and honor, and that it has been possible to tell them that they must behave honorably. And they stand quietly with their mother. Perhaps we will have to understand all this, and to understand how many people may be endangered in the present world.[1]

+ + +

Louis' Catullus: He has translated a dead language into a language which is powerless to be born. The contrast between the tone of Catullus and ^*some lines as*^ Louis' "I'll Go whee, and I'll rumble you" does nothing to lessen the comedy.[2]

This is a [ ] of one language with Catullus: the first ~~called dead~~ ^a "dead language"^; the new powerless to be born"[3]

The wide spread anti-semitism among Negroes is Uncle Tomism raised to the level of viciousness. One helps a white gentle man open his car door, or one helps a white gentleman beat up immigrants. Equally sycophantic

+ + +

They used to advise young men to avoid gambling, drink and women.

And they were probably right in their time. But the single most important thing in the world today is not to read the New Yorker.

If a man looks about him at all, which is to say, if he appears as a new poet at all, he is bound to be in some sense local.

Tomlinson, for all that he is influenced by the Americans, and means to be, is a very English poet. More aware of "a peopled landscape"[4] Less aware than we might be of the curvature of the earth.

+ + +

of course they are even entitled to equality. They have a perfect right to go to hell with us since they want to. And since they certainly know nowhere else to go anyway.

the art world has become the perfect duplication of the world of the industrial concerns together with the money of the industrialists
last years model valueless, etc.

To know what's DOING IN ORDER NOT TO DO WHATS BEING DONE OR HAS BEEN DONE. as rezi should have read the Imagists—to avoid some things that he might better have avoided

to see the child as substantial, as a person.

language again

error to see the "successful" as "real," ^*then abandon the real world*^ and failure as the pre-real, as the childish.

Creeley finally largely mannerist   one remembers the manner, not the poem

and the failure of people   one sees the land lying beneath the sun the more clearly.

"again the form at rest is the defining limit of intelligence, and intelligence is the notion of the form, so that all are one"
Plotinus

the infant first sees, not objects, but being

the world moves
and remains

The overwhelming intellectual force of Rome—armed with the Greek, and finally the Hebrew also

the old man's head,[5] ~~impenetrable~~ ^*bulging*^
And worn
Almost to death, ~~bulging~~
It grows ~~intolerable~~ from within
and is eroded

If poetry is an instrument of thought, and a fairly powerful one, he cannot simply put his convictions into verse. And therefore he takes some risks.

NOT the risk of technical innovation. What risk? except of having to
re-write perhaps   at worst
the risk is something else

+ + +

because here
because there is no visible force called chance we encounter
They said they were the people of the book, and i added a people
who possessed a literature of such power in that day

Plaque
In the cemetery of Pere Lachaise[6]
history beginning with the voice   —I am what is"

To the ten thousand
with the Jew also something or someone by the name
of Jehovah.

the sense will not close. Whereas the mind works intermittently. therefore the "merely intellectual" etc and the irreality of necessary truth. a time may have other tasks than poetry Why not But refrain from tearing up the roots, from injuring the roots

when words achieve meaning it is an important moment in my life and I do not usually forget it

But it is we who reason

they are destroyed by the passage of time. But there is something not destroyed . . .

lighting a corner of a table
and a chair
in a culture so mined and cultivated etc[7]

the lines are an instrument
of thought, ~~powerful~~
^*powerful*^ as the tools
of ~~the mathematician~~ *mathematics*
or they are distraction

the lines being an instrument of thought, one cannot ~~always~~ foresee conclusions, as the mathematician cannot
foresee the result of his work

Being, in which intelligence must come to rest. The defining limit of thought[8]

+ + +

He who makes and assembles   or from pure air
and his passion
makes

form   the completed act of the intellect

the old regime in the last days turns to terror, and therefore all the new are heroes

the mind from a world of whirling particles produces form

we cannot continue to celebrate the heroism of non-participation.
obviously a gag

under the roofs of Paris the young gather. A deliberate undertaking life force? is the aesthetic traceable to the evolutionary process? an ideal?
a life force?   under the roofs of paris, etc

Sisyphus, the moment of choice, Of freedom, of the concern of being

the idea that "occurs"—"it occurred to me"

the beauty of the Seine
At night

which perhaps does not matter
And nothing will come of it

and a new excitement rises
As the colored lights go on at night
In the cafes

 of structure
Closed by their slate roof
And complete, a culture

Mined and cultivated
From the ground[9]

+ + +

The problem of purpose and the problem of self-sufficiency—
irreconcilable

the universe itself given a god, a ruler, whose will it does.
which leaves god in his turn something which "does not know
but only acts"
the self sufficient vz. purpose

my lines and the division of lines is not meant merely as a cadence of sound. It is an essential element of the syntax.

+ + +

Newtonian rationalist particles motivated by an outside force, and the source of that force cannot be rationally found. Nor escaped, neither found nor escaped, it brings us only to determinism. And the idea of an intrinsic force is vitalism, and mysticism?

A force inherent in substance?
Or else in an entity <u>*outside*</u> *of substance?*

—I believe in something like natural
childbirth. To know, as far as one can face it,
what happens.

the song of songs—that one song, at least, in almost all lives

He who cannot wiggle, cannot love. An undignified thought. I mean to maintain intelligence and the clarity of intelligence even as an acknowledgment, if we can do no more, or tragedy, of human failure

one might well give one's whole poetic life to achieving that clarity had Rezi not already achieved it. So one tries to get deeper. At some loss Rezi's whimsicality of posture, occasionally, perhaps to palliate the tragic vision of materialism
as is his nationalism.

+ + +

It is approximately the distinction between a poem and an essay. A man, finding himself in possession of a number of opinions which he would like to express, writes an essay

an explorer or a mathematician also knows what he thinks—but doesn't know what he will find   a man applying a method of thought as which is powerful in itself, which is more powerful than the ordinary forms of discourse, doesn't know what he will find, or what he will think
Then

the man who refuses labor has decided in advance not to love
I could not have invented this, this I found

Plotinus———Mind, remembering will say   it was within, and yet it was not within

had won exaltation and life—surely of all things in literature
the most hard won where nothing is won easily

The People, the People   would it be so objectionable to say to
the people;   if you reject the radical intellectual, you will rot

the idea of being hovers over a dream more clearly than over waking
thought as over the fact of failure *(in Bernard's ULYSSES)*[10]
"the Muse" —— the feminine principle? why not say so?

no beginning and no end but only an interminable middle

searching for an invention
which will make them artists
and leave behind the field and ^*or* [   ] *or the streets*^ roads of
the   country
and the scenes of humiliation
and their non emotion

the universe however is nowhere
the self sufficient the impenetrable, the morally meaningless

The failure to believe
In science or mathematics
And failure of emotion—

One <u>is forced</u> to assume that the universe is absolutely self-sufficient. And cannot be eternally meaningless. Are one's own purposes an ethic?

+ + +

Spiritualism as a search for mystification is a game, and a ridiculous one. It is difficult to imagine boredom so great that one would play it.

No materialist philosophy can avoid the picture of life as tragic, and the history of life as absolute tragedy, because all life can neither tolerate ^*an ending nor*^ the thought of unendingness, ~~nor the thought of an end~~. And because if the universe is matter, it is impenetrable.

The suggestion of spiritual entities in the universe is a search, or a hope, of intelligibility. If it is not that, its simply a preference for confusion. ^*And confusion is*^ *perhaps a farce rather than tragedy.*

+ + +

If we were born, full blown, in space, a planet hanging enormously in front of *us,* ~~it seems to me that~~ no one ~~w~~could hunt for misty words or for "mysticism." One would say Look! Or, do you see it? or What is it? I should suppose that nothing—nothing at all—but the constant repetition of abstract words could blind us to that presence—

the designer reading the trade journals for the latest word is not going to produce a new art. Nor the young people reading the poets ^*most*^ in the news—

At 16 I was reading not Edna Millay nor the novelist Hutchinson, but the Anatomy of Melancholy, and Locke, and Keats—[11]

"Since there is a God he must—" Because if there were not God there would be no religion. Scientific argument: Since there is not a teleology—roughly speaking, a God, then what must have happened is———followed by an hypothesis as difficult to believe as Darwinism. Because IF there were a teleology, there would be no science. Therefore, since—etc. But the argument for neo Darwinism reduces itself always to no more than that: "since—then there must—"

Whose mind moves
Always toward those limits

We fear that grief
Which will render everything meaningless,
The sense of self among the motor cars
Meaningless:
We are an old race. That is,
There have been a lot of us.

+ + +

"as a necessary consequence of its own existence" Plotinus[12]

"the lower world of becoming was not created at a particular moment but is eternally generated" Plotinus

"Each must give of its own being to something else. The Good will not be the Good . . . Soul will not be Soul unless. . . . some secondary life lives as long as the primal exists"

"all things must exist for ever in ordered dependence on each other"

+ + +

Because this generation appears after the emergence ^*again*^ of *a* "new poetry"—the Beats or the black mountain or whatever name one wishes to use—appears when the argument of the schools emerges again after it has been absent for a short time, and because of the absurd speculation in the art galleries which causes it to appear that a man may think of using stripes, or serial images or blank spaces and become a great artist—or an artist at all—it is necessary to say what should be obvious; that it is impossible for a man to become an artist by having an idea, by making an invention. Art can come only from a very dangerous thing to do. To search for the roots of one's own existence and one's own sensibility. And to try to body that forth, to cause it to appear in clarity—

———

"of course"——meaning, it follows from the course of events, from the course of the argument. That on the course established one is bound to some, to this conclusion without the necessity of excursion—

—owed to Theodore Sturgeon) an "absolute ethic," meaning of course a human ethic—Determined by the requirements of the survival of humanity. An action may be ethical within a group, or ethical in terms of the survival of the group, but unethical in terms of the survival of humanity. A possible ethical basis for the Nuremberg trials——which ~~had~~ ^*offered*^ none.

The prophet conceit?"—not a myth, but a paradox

"We have scotch'd the snake, not killed it
She'll turn and be her selfe[13]
the wholeness of woods

+ + +

I am talking of a being

I am not ~~talking of~~ ^*displaying*^ a dialectic. I am talking of a vision.
Only I am talking of any vision. *of all vision*

but while I live I will speak, and while I have
reason I must answer.
11 Esdras

The similarity is that he is pretty young— one finds himself armed with some strength of character—one may have felt it precisely as one feels a sword at his side or to be flourished in the hand—one comes finally to think of even the armament of his own character as pure luck, a gift from god knows where—

When it becomes conviction it becomes poetic—and nothing but conviction is poetry

"your own things that grow up with you, you cannot understand
11 Esdras[14]

Nor does anything perish except that which can be transformed into something else; that which has nothing into which it can be transformed does not perish Plotinus

Might—like I—translate Ou sont les neiges d'antan[15]
as Who sent less needed eggs, Anton?

NOT A DIALECTIC
BUT VISION.—Not a dialectic
But vision . . .

I am speaking of the streets
Tho I know that if the universe is matter
It is impenetrable—

+ + +

Behold——not rainbow, which is mist—the full word.[16]
To see a grain of sand in the world, an hour out of eternity.[17]

a [stre]tch of vast river showing— hard to get to—not water, oil on the surface—current—the ship—a steel wall; barnacles and rivets—cannot see (in the wind) pressed against the steel wall hard shoes on
heres miracle with burnt matchstick

The hand, we use the hand for holding
Legs for walking
The car he gears
But the eye looks and we SEE, it floods in on us across the broad grey water to Jersey tangled in the grey air. *Penetrating, twisted, hard,*
(grey in the grey air)
irregular
Brick in the wall, the heart seizes it because the eye has picked it *out*[18]
the little lumps make it oneself.

[ ] hill and farm house—home to the eye—or the brass plate in the apt house lobby.

A young man running the ^*freight*^ elevator
Furious. Or in leather gloves
handling garbage, a few years out of high school
Thrown into primacy, ~~who were children among adults~~
~~And already failures~~ ^*They were children*
among adults
And already failures^
—cut off from
—the young, the disappointed.
No one will stand for it. No one

Trailer camps, the gadgets.
Row boat—of new wood as old as carpentry
Remember from before our birth
Stem meets the water perfectly—dipping a little, meets the
  water perfectly each time

Passenger, stowaways—you know you are the stowaways
since you are not fish—we must define life and freedom to
include the crew

The eye searches to see more

Rounding the buoy—the wind over the water
The boat moves more lightly ~~with the wind~~ *with the wind*
I call the thin planks, the light wood
And remember
To shore—for the sea is only the sea
And the beach a playground for children
To the shore, carpenter—
carpenter and other things
For the sea is only the sea We do not live by the sea

the sea—spatial simplicity—close to the boat the sea is water—in the
shadows of the boats side becomes suddenly water

+ + +

On the difficulty of advising or appraising a young poet, a poet who has not yet achieved mastery of his own form.

had I seen Ginsberg's Kadish in the making, I would have wanted to strike out almost every phrase, almost every line. It is the poem that justifies the line, not the lines that justify the poem. It is the poem that justifies the words.

+ + +

Now the Now

Those little islands of existence in the city—a streetlamp, an iron fence, a subway station which Rezi saw in the city with so much love are also overawing. They exist at the same time uncompromisingly—and so they seem at the same time to exist uncompromisingly and to be lost

Father, father
Of fatherhood
Who haunts us, suffering
Man most naked
Of us all, O father[19]

We can keep nothing, but can give everything
———"use up"

Pragmatism. . . . . that we cannot judge the reasonableness or logic of our reason except by the result of actions

The condition of humans, of occupants of a planet

May no armure hit lette, ne none hye walles[20]

The society—Of course I dislike it, we all dislike it. That is its quality. It has forced and at the same time made possible the creation of ridiculous thousands of artists. Obviously a dangerous thing for a society to do, and I have little idea what will come of it.

the opposite of a Republic

We get into arguments which are obviously competitive, a competition for the market. Different people have different purposes. They make what they want to make

+ + +

We must cease to believe in secret names and unexpected phrases which will burst the world. Neither the rational mind nor the free action of the nerves of the mind will disclose anything beyond their experience. The rational mind has this capacity, however: that it is able to perceive the limits of knowledge, and thereby ~~to give reality to the things which are perceived~~ *to attest in reality—to the things that are perceived*

+ + +

Actually, to adopt the super-militant program of the Black Muslims is to decide not to face police dogs, police clubs and jails and beatings in the South.

in the kind of thinking which is literature, as in mathematics, one does not bother to write down a problem of which he already knows the answer.

to write down what he can "do in his head."

Odd that one believes in Caesar easily enough
But not one's father's childhood—

Some kind of desperation
That he could not bear ten words
Without a punch line;

Unable to speak without ~~an~~ epigrams
He carried something like a vaudeville act
Thru the little city of San Francisco, and finally
Thru half the watering places of Europe[21]

+ + +

Whitman. Dirge for two veterans: The key is the phrase "the great convulsive drums". With that phrase, something happens, beyond that phrase two things are going on simultaneously, one of which is a very bad poem. The other is not.[22]

Disheartening to suppose the time will never come when everyone is materially right, well-off. But if that day does arrive, the human race will be ethically and intellectually unemployed—there will be no "higher values." Is that right? is that what one thinks?

In ~~literature~~ "literary" thought, as in mathematics, what you can do in your head you don't bother to write on paper.

In the kind of thought which is literary thought, or the kind of thought which is more than precious literature, as in mathematical thought,

Actually, to ~~endorse the Muslims in their uncompromising militancy is to decide to do nothing.~~ adopt the super-militant position of the Black Muslims is to decide <u>not</u> to fight police dogs, clubs, jails

in the south

+ + +

Things have already happened before I was here

The jews, thru their concern of others, their social and political, their ethical involvements, have very nearly destroyed themselves. Puritanism, anti-aestheticism which tends to leave them for their indulgence only luxuriousness, display—

+ + +

To regard political involvement as a kind of suicide?
To "give one's life" to it, as indeed they say? As: a man finds himself given an actual opportunity to save the lives of the Jews in the German concentration camps. Could he not do it? And why? The common phrase is "I have to live with myself," but that explains nothing.

But this is seldom the case. It can happen in effect that one says, I cannot anyway live in a world in which such things happen . . . or in which that has happened. Therefore with any odds against   This would be a form of suicide, or suicide barring some slight hope of success. No. What is thought of is an eventual success, which will not take place, or is less likely to take place without his sacrifice, and if no effort is made, if the greatest possible effort is not made, he doesn't wish to live—or doesn't wish to be human.

Trapped
In work, they dream
Of profit

time: the life of the mind.

+ + +

a man of sixty—. He remembers rather easily the events ~~of the day~~ ^*which occurred*^ when he was forty. ~~It has~~ ^*They have*^ one of the mystery of the remembrance of childhood. Twenty years therefore seems a short time to him. But in twenty years he will be dead. A man in a death cell, awaiting ~~for~~ execution—one expects that all his thoughts will include the thought of death.

One simple viewpoint—which is not whether physics—past, present, future, near, far, matter & movement—is philosophy. Ancient philosophy developed before men became man? And UNTRUE. Incorrect.

We share or have shared a philosophy—of fact, premise—with the higher animals. Our language is built on it. And probably will change   A different language

| *another viewpoint—[   ] and the convex mirror. She does not move.* |

<u>*TIME—TIME—*</u>
Yes, I know, the moral's really less unnatural. The people he wanted acknowledge a lord. This seems really it.

+ + +

Time is the life of the soul ((mind?)) in movement.   Plotinus

The movement of MIND is the autism of mind? It seems credible

paraphrasing Plotinus: there was ((or there developed))
“a nature” which wished to grow, to seek. “This moved,” and so created time.   III.7.II[23]

The inveterate New Yorker—she cannot begin at the beginning. The beginning to her is mere sordidness. She is over it as quickly as possible[24]

+ + +

One must assume the world
~~is morally inert~~
is self-sufficient
absolutely and ~~therefore~~ morally inert,
^*Therefore.*^ And one’s own purposes
An ethic   ethic: ethos
Morals; mores   what other words
Can be found? Awe,
perhaps—
Which is not
“Ethical”

We assume the physical world is morally inert & morality therefore represents one’s own purposes.

Something about failure—the idea of being hovers over the face of failure   hovers more clearly over the face of failure than over the brilliance of success. The successful: a parade of scarecrows.

flattery in dignity

the necessity to draw back   to be a little “out”   to become aware of . . . .

Necessary truth———the mediaeval bestiaries.

+ + +

it is possible to make use of words provided one treat them as the enemy. Or ^*perhaps*^ not the enemy—. Wild beasts which have run mad in the subways ^*the department stores, the banks*.^ If one ~~takes~~ ^*captures*^ them one by one, and proceeds very carefully, it is possible to restore them to meaning.[25]

If a poem—if verse—is something more than an elocutionary device, it tends to final conclusions—

The universe surely is
morally inert?   And one's own
purposes . . .

But I assume the physical universe. The extant universe—is morally inert

+ + +

Plato a consistent distinction between actuality and—something else. Not only in the metaphysics, of course, but at the heart of every argument. "Then the ruler, as ruler, will rule justly." ~~^Surely^ such a statement has nothing to do with the nature of any ruler or of any institution of rulership, and nothing to do with the nature of fact. I would think it an arid fantasy.~~

It seems to me a fantasy. ~~*The fantasy of a ruler ruling as a ruler, not as himself but as a ruler*~~

The Kennedy anthology:[26]

I rather think of verse as a tool of thought, perhaps comparable to the tool of mathematics. Admittedly the comparison suffers strain. But I find that tho I might well write a poem to test the truth of a common assumption, I would not write simply to give thrilling tongue to a common belief than I would work a sum for the same purpose. *I do not think that poetry is merely a type of creation.*

the civil rights ~~issue~~ anthology[27]——I am far from wishing to join the current ^*prevalent*^ claim for inaction as a form of heroism. But there is a difficulty. ^*It is perhaps*^ the difficulty of promising human happiness, above all of promising human happiness as a result of achieving parity with "us." If a poem is something more than an elocutionary device, it tends toward final conclusions ______________________

Clear cold space
Between us
There is man—A relative life
In which men never lived
Not as living now—

Destruction means——to open our ears.
Heid. What is Philosophy page 73[28]

a fact— he means to destroy himself

\+ + +

We have uttered the word "philosophy" often enough. If, however, we use the word "philosophy" no longer like a worn out title, if, instead, we hear the word "philosophy" coming from its source, then it sounds thus: philosophie. Now the word philosophy is speaking Greek. The word, as a Greek word, is a path.

Heidegger, What is Philosophy page 29

I think always about the thing in which we are. Among the things in it is force, power. It is not enough to say that we like it or that we do not like it. It is here, we must first talk about it. We are not shoppers—or we are not first of all shoppers; it is not enough to say that we like or we do not like—

E's piece in Harper's:

Galleons, not boats; Sultans not men with a lot of stuff—an inability to begin at the beginning, a lack of substance. The New Yorker, who knows nothing and never can know anything. The shopper, the chooser, *the talker.*

She has taken the way of saving herself that all of these people have taken who have saved themselves at all. To learn, to know something, to be scholars. But there is nothing she can know. June is lucky to be a Westerner. What she does learn she knows, as we do, in a realistic way, as something added to the vision of the bare ground, as something added to the bare fact of being alive.

Brutality is a beginning: preciousness is an end.

Came to N.Y.   which needed nothing more!

E's anger listening to David, anger at being forced to listen to David—. He is a Russian Jew![29]

The problem is to be someone. Or rather the problem is that one always is. E who has listened to Japanese sages and to Indian Gurus—cannot listen to a Russian Jew!

one dislikes it still to quote a caterpillar,
But the important thing is: Begin at the beginning.[30]

+ + +

I write about things which may be abstractions to many people.
I don't write about them if they are abstractions to me.

. . . but you will not write differently when you are fifty six?
Williams remained extraordinarily young, but Williams' death was a terrible one because it was a boy dying. That survival of youth is not the only way to last well, and perhaps not the best way.

"What books would you choose to have with you on a desert island?"

"My own."

****

the
the the

Seems to me to mean that truth is empirical.
Which is Aquinas' Veritas sequitur esse rerum. A
statement which seems to me, by a kind of poetic process,
a process of remembering ~~one's own experience, inescapable.
As I recall it,~~ I found the thing. The world could have
been different in any respect. Including 'circles'.
Or one's habit of imagining circles.

I can see nothing at all except that one
encounters the thing. And, it is impossible not to say,
encounters oneself. ~~For which the conditions were also
present, were [illegible] also a "given."~~
And encounters in
himself the passion of logic which, like the young
man's desire to sleep with Debbie Reynolds, is unlikely
to be satisfied, but can lead to crimes of violence.

Tho I am not altogether opposed to crimes
of violence, as you must know, since I am not altogether
pleased by the idea of standing still. And the logical
passion may be unique in this. I mean, young men might
still be wishing to sleep with the neolithic Venus, if
the matter were left to the less progressive passions .

Goedel has proven that the neothlithic venus
is either incomplete or contradictory. I hesitate to
say that he has demonstrated anything of the sort concerning
Debbie Reynolds.

But time will show.

[Just means truth is
empirical: has to be
encountered]

Daybook III

From Oppen's "Nailed Daybook," papers bound to small block of wood by means of a single nail. As with the "Stapled Daybook" and the "Pipe-Stem Daybooks," the "Nailed Daybook" contains drafts of letters and poems (excised), as well as the following notes. Likely bound after the completion of the manuscript for *Of Being Numerous,* although resonance with letters from the early to mid-1960s (see notes) suggest that some of the reflections were recorded much earlier.

+ + +

On the pervasive contemporary pragmatism: the assumption that a statement that does no good ~~is not true~~ is useless, is not true.

Eastern thought: necessarily within the Western, and in the Christian tradition at least since Plotinus. And in fact much earlier. The Vedanta's are not an ^*esoteric*^ revelation to the Westerner who has read Western philosophy. The point is rather the Heidegerrian idea that all peoples burst into history with these thoughts first burst into history with these thoughts. And that all people, all persons, reaching any profundity of thought, are aware of these things.

"A flight of the alone to the Alone" Plotinus: Enneads. Soul is indivisible, all souls are one. The soul does not inhabit the world, but the world is in the soul. i.e. the one and indivisible soul. The soul neither comes into being nor perishes.[1]

SUTRA = "Thread" (from Sanskrit)

later Sutra probably from Sanskrit)

+ + +

Now one might form an "opinion" in such areas. But as I recall it, I found the thing. It seems to me that the world could have been different in any respect. Including circles. Or one's habit of imagining circles.

I can see nothing at all except that one encounters the thing. And, it is impossible not to say, encounters oneself. And encounters in himself the passion of logic which, like the young man's desire to sleep with the latest movie star, is unlikely to be satisfied, but can lead to crimes of violence.

$x^2 = y$

———

If there is something there, there is <u>one</u>. If there is something elsewhere, there is <u>two</u>. If there is nothing, there is zero. But there are no twos or threes.[2]

+ + +

Seems to me to mean that truth is empirical.
Which is Aquinas' Veritas sequitur esse rerum. A statement which seems to me, by a kind of poetic process, a process of remembering one's own experience, inescapable.

> As I recall it, I found the thing. The world could have been different in any respect. Including "circles."
>
> Or one's habit of imagining circles.

I can see nothing at all except that one encounters the thing. And, it is impossible not to say, encounters oneself. ~~For which the conditions were ^also^ prudent, were ^also given^~~

And encounters in himself the passion of logic which, like the young man's desire to sleep with Debbie Reynolds, is unlikely to be satisfied, but can lead to crimes of violence.

Tho I am not altogether opposed to crimes of violence, as you must know, since I am not altogether pleased by the idea of standing still. And the logical passion may be unique in this. I mean, young men might still be wishing to sleep with the neolithic Venus, if the matter were left to the less progressive passions.[3]

Gödel has proven that the neolithic Venus is either incomplete or contradictory. I hesitate to say that he has demonstrated anything of the sort concerning Debbie Reynolds.[4]

But time will show.

Just means that truth is empirical, has to be encountered

+ + +

The simple fact: art is <u>not</u> good for us.

"Thought consists in a search for truth: life in a "search for advantage" Yesenin-Volpin.[5] *They are not necessarily separable. We have been lucky with science—with physics, astronomy, even cosmology—we may not be so lucky with either art or with philosophy. It is the assumption that the luck is inevitable that creates the unexamined pragmatist assumption of almost all modern thought.*

An answer:

> *it is possible to conceive of god making*
> *the universe; it is impossible to conceive of the*
> *universe making god.*

+ + +

certainly the growth of liberalism in this country has saved my life—and I would not attempt to live in an illiberal country—unless perhaps in an underground. If I am cantankerous toward liberals, it is probably because I am cantankerous. And also because if we can assume for moments at a time that liberalism is fairly secure— or even if we cannot, I would want to say that we cannot live our whole lives in pure self-defense—. Which I think is what the liberal positions amount to. Not more. i.e., the status quo—the status which exists at least for us

+ + +

poets, artists—such people—really do not mean to share the generally accepted virtues. They mean to make new ones. Of course, they may fail—I think perhaps they will—I mean altogether, and right now—soon. In which case I think you'll find that human life becomes unbearable fairly soon. But it may happen all the same.

Thought . . . gropes
In time   :

I, says the buzzard,
I—[6]

+ + +

The desire for immortality, ted[7]

The desire for luxury, the desire for immortality—
one as crude a desire as the other.

<table>
<tr><td>Flat plain
and the flat road

“In my father’s house”</td><td>The flat plane
of history
in my father’s house
Is only this?</td></tr>
</table>

Is only this?

(no more than this?)

“At whose behest does the mind think?”
Upanishads

I imagine men living in a dreadful society in which no man sailed a little boat in order to be on the sea or walked in the country in order to walk. Sitting in a boat moved by hired rowers, he imagined nothing better than that there should be more, or more vigorous rowers, or richer decorations, or softer pillows, or still softer women. And found no escape from such desires but to "look inward," and to substitute the greed of immortality for the other greeds.

But a bare table—. One is aware of space above it.
of space, in fact, around it, and unlimited space—?

Or are they really cowardly?

Euphoria somehow connected with time as essential to it—the time ahead?—"Happy that they existed"

"Appearance represents and mis-represents reality"   Heid.
ie.   indicates the real.

The gallows speech: a few years' difference for us.

The old gardens: But it is only a little place, you see. Little things can [ ] them

Heidegger: Man creates not <u>being</u>, but the *there* of being-there (Das Sein)

+ + +

Parousia

There is the one gap ^*in the mind*^, the space of the mind, in which everything may be held at arm's length, everything may be seen from outside, and in which the will moves.

Against the pressure of substance, that sanctuary cannot stand forever. Man will enter his Millennium, his Millennium of obsession, ~~or he will discard the human to be coeval with the planets as a race of engineers and calculators.~~

I am far from doubting the world. It can be seen, and it cannot be understood. And I believe that fact is lethal.

Surely language has not created the real, but has made it visible. We do not see if we are dazzled, dazed, confused, tho we hear when we hear confusedly and we feel if we feel at all. Submerged in the world, we hear and we feel; without a word we remember the taste of an apple.

At certain points, certain places, if one walks forward he steps into water. With ^*speech and*^ the word, ~~we know~~ it is the sea, we see the sea.

If we are able to imagine the world from outside, we see that it was our home.

I think language is art, is poetry, the violent poetry of love and of possession of the real, and I suspect that it is lethal.[8]

+ + +

We are ^*are we not*^ the besieged and doomed sanctuary—the space of the mind—which is able to hold everything at arm's length, to see everything from outside? The pressures of substance and of eternity increase, /and that sanctuary cannot endure forever./ / /

+ + +

that man, the space of the mind, is a flaw, a gap, a besieged and doomed sanctuary which is able to hold ~~being~~ at arms length—

I am far from believing that it does not exist. I believe that it exists, that it cannot be understood, that that fact is lethal, ~~and that man will not exist forever~~ and that there can be no help for us.

The most violent, who cannot be helped, who smash that empty bubble of the mind against the absolute solidity of being.

The flaw, the gap which is aware of being, tho it is within it. The flaw on which being presses.

If we are able to imagine ourselves outside, we see that it was our home.

Being, the being of substance and of eternity.

He is, as they say, creative, Which is pure violence.

We are the besieged and doomed sanctuary—the space of the mind—which is able to hold everything at arm's length ^*the pressures of substance of eternity increase, and the sanctuary cannot hold forever*^, and which cannot endure forever the pressures

of substance and of eternity increase.

Least of all we who are, as they say, creative, which is pure violence.

Language is poetry in that it creates reality, or ^*that it*^ makes it visible. We say we hear, tho we hear confusedly, but we do not say that we see if we are dazzled, dazed, *confused*—

At a certain point we step into water.

With the word, we know it is the sea, we see the sea. *From outside it.*

Without the word, we can feel as if from the inside. The taste of an apple, the sensation of sunlight—With the word, we see, *we see from outside.*

+ + +

"This in which" all truth is contained—all that is true is contained

We force a path
Everywhere in fear of finding
Nothing—   strangers
~~Who fear~~
The strangeness of death

Less than anyone are we secure in order, because we create order it cannot contain us—

as tho we have invented knowledge?

if a man ceases to think of himself as a part of history he must think of himself on the same plane as other animals

"The question of what man is must always be taken in its essential bond with how it stands with being"—Heidegger, Metaphysics, page 118

O, they will say such things! Lizards with red tails, tennis balls that walk! Whoo—the mind of cannot sustain it, we will run mad!

+ + +

The indian—because he has his song, he knows himself, can hold his manhood—We read this as something which they had, but behind it is the description of precariousness, of awareness of the abyss, of proximity to the abyss greater, possibly, than ours. The people of absolute security—we cannot understand. If in fact they spoke of the Swedish Chronicles[9]

who is the Roman soldier he is being—what is the picture in his mind—Roots, we have roots, we have roots everywhere and in every century, but wonder if they are ours—how are they ours—? The pictures we live by. All but our own? "We walk about on the earth until we drop"   the need to extend back in time, the fact that we do, the picture in the mind—

why archetype? or when?

When. Could it be imagined?

the historic past clear enough. We say, but these people felt alone. Alright. But having found the word "alone" we understand everything.

+ + +

To perceive . . . . . .
Is to stand on the edge
. . . . to recognize
contingency

+ + +

The young sculptor[10]
Who lives near us

Told me: I had a dream
And in the dream I asked someone
What is a poet? And whoever it was

Said, a poet
Is a man
Who goes in the world

Naked. And people who have forgotten
How to feel

Come to him, and he holds them
Until they can feel again.

+ + +

I think that if one is not dealing with the perspective of his life at all—if one is not thinking of what a man might ultimately want of himself or of his life, but is simply trying to deal with an immediate problem, to do a job, to adjust to something which he cannot or does not want to exclude from his life—the Freudian does not want to exclude from his life—the Freudian analysis

But it has little to do with what anyone—now—believes that he wants of himself—

One goes to a doctor when he is ill: one lives by a philosophy. Psycho-analysis is a therapy. But a philosophy which is not a search for truth: is—as philosophy—condemned to dishonesty from the root.

What I cannot bare—I speak of[11]

In the beginning was   Truth—intelligible law,
                necessary truth

Conquest of the void—and they are welcome

The poetry depends on the knowledge of being alone, & yet of exactly another history—

Aeolian —	*C*
Dorian —	*D to D*
Phrygian —	*E to E*
Lydian —	*F to F*
Ionic	*A to A*

+ + +

Cummings:

There is no doubt that he invented some most ingenious little machines of poems. What injures those poems is the unfathomable stupidity of the man, and the weary, weary, increasingly weary little self-congratulatory statement those machines tinkle out. What they mean to say is that Cummings feels as simple and pure a delight in many things as he feels for candy, the point being that Cummings is a most entrancing child-man. As a statement of actual admiration for people, scenes, events, their insincerity is unmistakable.

+ + +

<u>Intelligence</u>   consists
In permitting
Disorder to enter
Your world
From the world

+ + +

Thus the primordial intuition of being is the intuition of the solidity and inexorability of existence; and second, of the death and nothingness to which MY existence is liable. And third, in the sane flash of intuition, which is but my becoming aware of the intelligible existence, perceived in anything whatsoever, implies. I do not yet know in what form, perhaps in the things themselves, perhaps separately from them—some absolute, irrefragable existence, completely free from nothingness and death. these three leaps

Maritain[12]

Le Balcon—[13]

Someone shot Kennedy, why? He wanted to play the part. Ruby shot Oswald: he wanted to play that part, and we want to play the parts . . . saying, There <u>*wasn't*</u> *anything else to do. [ ]*

+ + +

I have said before—but there seems nothing essential to add.

I think of literature not as a part of the entertainment industry, but as a process of thought. I think of the image—not the "imagery," but the image produced by the poem as a test of truth, or at least of conviction. A test, in the end, of attitudes, a final validation of thought;

If a man should get to the moon on his own contraption, he will know how he feels about it. It may depend on circumstances whether or not the public regards him as a great man.

Duncan: suggests art as an adventure, not as achievement.[14]

+ + +

therefore none of the question alter?   beyond any real question we learn by substance that which exists the coming together of views which has so excited the spiritualist has actually derived from their vocabulary of meaning. They are excited at the moment by the fact that the physical is no longer clearly separated from what they have considered spiritual. They have somehow failed to understand therefore.

the error is a peculiar consequence inherent from the beginning—

That "the world is becoming invisible"[15]

means that it is the world which is becoming invisible, not some "other" world.

I wanted that poem to seem perfectly clear—in marching order—and to wind itself nowhere. Therefore I wrote it in iambics. And because it is in iambics——   the New Yorker took it.

WHEN i write another poem in iambics—
I'll send it.[16]

finally realize——

Sticking a fencing sword into a gut was not what Steve was trying to do in the first place![17]

+ + +

Someone makes the picture, and cuts the jigsawed pieces, and dumps them out on the table—and then you can play the game! Masterfully. But they could have been other pieces—

I have by now clearly got a step, or half a step, beyond the Materials

perhaps beyond the materials. I was wrong insofar as I imagined that I would take a turn and see another horizon. If I have seen another horizon I cannot understand it yet.

+ + +

and, as fifty million philistines, who can't be wrong, have taken the trouble to argue out, it isnt quite true that "one writes for oneself"

The effect of rime derives from the fact that it is the repetition of a note—Of a pitch

There are also fifths, and there are probably octaves.

Making me figure out
Ten million *obvious*
~~Obvious~~

   Things for them/ and I can't say/
The thing is you won't live long
Anyway
   the thing is to see where you are
While you are—

So I talk to them

~~The poem~~: One feels fear
and must react in fear,

[ ]. That is the poem

+++

I mean my work to be a process of thought. Which means I am the literary equivalent of the scientist. not of the [ ]—not, that is to say, the entertainer.

+++

prosody:

The line of poetry appears as a single foot which
centers around some point in the line

It does not seem that the human should could sustain eternity

Came, therefore, teleology the unspeakable name.

Obscurity, and the indignities of obscurity. And
the greater indignities *of prominence*

Movie making is only movie making, but many poets are poets

+ + +

Molier's gentleman was correct in discovering that he had been speaking prose all his life. Had he written it down, however, it would not have been more, but merely less.[18]

+ + +

There can be a brick
In a brick wall
The eye picks

So quiet of a Sunday,
And the continent
Lying under all of it[19]

no history of pre-metaphysical man.
Not a history, but a description of the events of mechanics.
"A history of a Penny": the penny is made conscious of being.

Have always written of clouds.

Dostoyevsky's phrase, then everything is permitted!
And Bergman's corollary: anything can happen.[20]

That man was neither more nor less natural
Than we. Like us, he was a product of evolution.

Rousseau was assuming, or wrote as if he assumed, that there was a primary man who appeared complete, absolutely untouched by experience, and by human society, from the hands of the creator, and that therefore that man was the natural man, modified by all developments beyond that first moment.[21]

—complete as man, and somehow or other moved man—
TO
A Narrative

+ + +

My "symbols"—I do not quite agree that they are symbols. The man who holds in his mind some rare thing—a crocus, an owl—and uses it to state a meaning has indeed found himself a symbol. But I speak of the things I see, and that I see everyday, because my life is led among them, because I have no life free from them, and must obviously find meaning in them if I am to find meaning. *at all.*

History of art: clearly Stevens interest could disappear. And Williams. I do not think Rilke or Blake could disappear. The statement is there, and cannot become hackneyed; it cannot be stated outside the poem. How much they may be "liked" at a given moment—but they are part of the history of perception.

exist historically

the relation of the man marooned, the man trapped, is that he is excluded.[22]

+ + +

(as in the story of an automobile):
It is possible to find in art witticism and even good advice, it is possible to find decorative qualities, pleasant sensations, ^*sustenance*^ ~~accounts which move one to sympathy or the desire to occupy an heroic role.~~ But the one thing which belongs to art is its ability to communicate the reality of experience, or the possible reality of experience. It is that which art does, it is that which is the purpose of art. It cannot be explained. People beat time to the waltz, and of course they enjoy it. A massage is probably even more enjoyable. It cannot be explained.

+ + +

story of the man living in a small city of the midwest who bought one of the first cars, and went to visit an uncle on his farm. The old man came out to see the automobile, of course, and got in when invited. Yes, he said, its real nice. I can see how come folks like them. From something about his tone the man realized that he didnt expect to be driven anywhere, and because he wasnt too anxious to take so old a man on a drive, he just sat beside him in the car. They sat a long while, until finally his uncle said he would have to go in. He said it was real nice. He said he saw that a car was a nice thing to have. Thought he might like to have one himself.

It might be a little hard for him, after that, ever really to understand the purposes of a car. It is not altogether irrelevant to judge a car by the comfort of the seats, so that it might never be possible to make him aware of the fact of power as the crucial factor in a car. One can imagine that people who began with such an attitude might finally travel quite a bit by car without ever really understanding. It would be quite natural to discuss whether or not the car was comfortable, it would be impossible to refuse to discuss that factor with them. And if one said something to them about the power, if one said the car did or did not have sufficient power, one can easily imagine that they might say simply that they didnt know much about those technicalities.

The precise word (Mary's) Kennedy was a creative man)

To see "the light of day," the passage of universal time—a necessity

The children sacrificing too much for the parent; a machine which consumes itself.

Perhaps a measure of intelligence is the awareness of disorder—

+ + +

To Steve)[23]

Classic liberalism, Sir Sir, with passion and with fury I will fight the Liberal Establishment.

I would hate to have to fight anything else.

Again.

Le Balcon: the first five scenes say something once and for all which should be fatal. But for our ability not to know that we are in fact dying of the wounds we have already received.[24]

not that all the world's a stage, but that, since the performance is for the pleasure of the actor, not the audience, it is a brothel. Shakespeare must stand corrected.

A man desires to undress a woman. In the same way, he wishes to assassinate a president, or to be a father, or to sacrifice his life for his country. And the acts, and the characters will be arranged, if one can command the social force—the price—to pay for the act.

As for "fatal" : as one reads he is excited, and even joyous, exhilarated, because he feels he is finding out !

This is the absolute paradox, which has so long made even the prospect of death supportable. "What we live for"

It desires to undress
a woman. ~~It is very strange~~

It desires—

Fatherhood, it desires
Praise

And fills a life—

We are grateful to Jacqueline Kennedy that she played a role so well for us. And perhaps she is fortunate that she was given a role to play, unlike the "little people" who find no role and no image.

The idea that one must have a role to play—

~~Perhaps the measure of intelligence is the ability to permit~~

+ + +

The wall, the wall adjoining together with the floor and the ceiling together with the furniture in the room and the people, sufficiently enlarged, would look precisely like the sky we see at night—

the "spiritual" experience is ^*not*^ ~~the sudden grasping~~ of the irrevocability of the real—

+ + +

. . . for several centuries the spiritual density of the true has become lighter than that of the false—

Maritain[25]

Possession of the earth

Since this door was intended only for you, I am now going to shut it.

Kafka[26]

a last day in which I have nothing
and nothing to suffer—

"Our Hello"—our greeting—Not over the familiar
extends, more threatening than elsewhere, the "over-
powering"

If we do not admit these things, if we deny or look away from these things, we abandon one another, we abandon all those in extremity, which is to abandon everyone finally—

Dick: "and by the wish to be an equal"   "the common
language"   also "invincible"

The Western dualism—because we have proven the expediency of logic, and have proven also its inability to reach truth—"things explain each other not themselves" the basis for unity. The eastern: Brahman spun the world for himself, as a spider produces a web. vs., in the beginning was—truth. Neither is the beginning——The only promise of the Christian system is—after death, the soul will know truth. *Because something is promised*

A whole world: who is Mr. Swann,
Who is Mrs. Swann, what are the harbors?[27]

The passions ~~establish~~   *(define)*
the good, and goodness

wills catastrophe, to emerge from the universe, to see the world from outside, total catastrophe, absolute destruction—

There is in the Christian system the possibility of despair, the event that breaks thru faith, the man curses god and dies—

+ + +

The mood by which any work ^*of art*^ is colored has been produced by the impact of simple events, things falling, air moving, the movements of living matter, a stone piled on a stone, something balanced momentarily—

"Everything is permitted":
    Anything can happen.

The echo of what is not homely—~~for example~~ ^*e.g.*^, the floor of a factory

The universe of laws, the lawless, arbitrary universe of laws.

+ + +

the

necessary truth is simply the "is" of discourse?

Because being is initially physis . . . it discloses itself as idea
    Heidegger[28]

the ~~arbitrary~~ abstract world of logic and precept and statement

not the thing, but its existence, not its "essence" but its existence

+ + +

I hoped then eventually to find a course of action which would create a discourse of imagism—certainly I had not done so then. The poems therefore are short, and perhaps fragmentary, and I think it may be

difficult to read them in a hall which is   large for such small poems.
But I will try—*I would like to try*

to know how to ask a question is to know how to wait, even a lifetime
Heid.[29]

+ + +

—with her childish
Goodness

Goodness, like a child's—

Defined by the passions
Of others, the needs

They were not told
to have

a whole world
here—Who is Mr. Swann

who is in the hospital?
Who is Mr. Swann?
What goes on
in the harbors,
on the piers?
Near the black tidal
Water? She creates

An abstract
Universe by the will

To be good, to be
Good like a child—

(others to their passions)

when a message has no clothes on,
How can it be spoken? Merton[30]

when a message is unclothed
cannot be clothed
    what touches
all edges, all boundaries, leaving no space
For clothing,
How can it be spoken?

And the dazed heart will

as man wills
and has always willed

catastrophe, to see
That world from outside

"If it had been possible to build the tower of Babel without ascending it, the work would have been permitted." (Kafka)[31] And has been, of course

Everything can be explained except truth.

+ + +

kids come out of high school—if they come out of high school with marks good enough to get into college—with a concept of themselves here, and knowledge as something out there from which they may handed facts as if over a counter. If they think of college as granting more freedom than high school, they think of something rather like a supermarket. It is necessary that they somehow come to get a glimpse of the production floor, of the workshop, where everything is a sort of mess, and everything might easily have been made quite differently

+ + +

An example:

We use the word "nature" as if it meant physical existence, physis, things. Natural science—physics—the study of things. And the word supernatural therefore seems to mean something which is above the nature of the world, a realm which is more real than reality, and at the same time not real at all, not "mere reality." But the words nature and natural and native do not derive from the word physis, but from the latin word which means born, and however we may mis-use the word, even speaking of "native-born," it is the root meaning which connects all clear meanings of the word. We believe that we can use the word, as we believe we can use any word, just as we please, and that its meaning is established by usage, including the hopelessly confused. But the word retains its root meaning until all meaning in the word has been destroyed. To be natural is to be as one was born to be; the natural world is the world as it was created. It is also the world which was created, as the supernatural is that which was not created but pertains to the eternal, to God. If one speaks of a supernatural event he probably means an intervention of Deity,

The point here being the preservation of words, of the meaning of words. The writers first concern is to be sure that he means anything, and for this he must preserve and restore the meaning of words. The dictionary merely records every possible mis-use of every word in the language.

Words get used badly, and destroyed. And continue to be used, and so destroy meaning and the possibility of meaning.

\+ + +

The word appearance—

"Don't be deceived by appearances" "He appears to be honest" "the ship appeared on the horizon"

The first treats "appearance" as contrasted with reality, ^*That meaning comes from*^ ~~the product of~~ bad philosophizing. A dictionary would include in ^*the meanings or usages of the word*^ appear and appearance a distinction from truth—It is not the dictionary's task to guard the language from meaninglessness. But it is the writer's first task to be certain that he means <u>anything</u>, *and for that purpose, he restores the meanings of words*

a poem——— probably avoid the words abstract and concrete. If one did use the word concrete, its meaning could be ~~restored to it~~ ^*guaranteed only*^ in a usage close to "specific"—tho the Oxford gives, among others, the meaning "every day"

A meaning derived from bad philosophizing and by now attached to the word itself in sufficiently sloppy speech. It is the dictionary's task to acknowledge what the user of a word might think he means by it, not to safeguard the language. But the writer must, first of all, be sure that he means anything. And so should anyone who means to speak seriously.

\+ + +

Yes, but I don't search for unexplained events. I ~~speak~~ think about what we all know. That it is a place. That there are things in it. That nothing enters it and nothing leaves it. That it is either infinite, or it ends somewhere. That it is either eternal, or it began sometime. If I wanted to write about the movement of tables, I would write a Physics. If I wanted to write about E*SP* I would write a Physiology. And if I thought I knew something of real estate values, I would write an investment guide. But I am not a physicist, nor a physiologist, nor an investment ~~councilor~~ banker. And I am not too interested in those things. I think that ~~it~~ ^*this*^ is a place. That there are things in it—. That is what I think about, and that is what I write about.

+ + +

perfection of tone, the perfect control of tone, but tone becomes the tone of comment and finally replaces respect for the world. It seems to be the pitfall of the woman poet.

and must choose between moralizing & caprice and fails, finally, of respect for the world. More reason to know the new woman poet—except Sappho—who has escaped

The whole which is
Holy at the root
Of the word
In the Anglo-Saxon
And of the word
Health, plentitude
Of being.
Wholeness, hale
And holy—

+ + +

The idea of eternity, the permanent—it is the source of religions.

This in which we are ~~seen~~ ^*understood*^ as everyone understands it: that it contains things which neither enter it nor leave it, that either it is infinite or ends somewhere, that either it is eternal or it began sometime—

That the words and the syntax are inapplicable, or that the words correspond to reality and the syntax to necessary truth and produce ~~a sentence which is~~ true ^*sentences*^ the content of which we cannot grasp.

Therefore, because, since, with its foolish
Sound, words
That we learned
As children twisting the new
Mouth, mimicking with the new
Tongue, words that the nurse
Used, a foreign
Heritage, and what words—*!*
How can they ^*that*^ force
One's hand!

The hereafter: what the children want!

+ + +

They imagined the idea of eternity—
imagined the necessary things of eternity, permanence—

a constant depth, or forget about it That is to say, if one does not need poetry, forget about it

As one might agree to forget for Platonic reasons—that the perfect state does not need poetry, and in fact will not permit it. It is not that which is terrible about the Communists, it is in fact not the open stringencies—which can be defended—but the liberal pretenses, the "let a thousand flowers bloom."[32] And it is these liberalisms, these dishonesties, which create the situation of total repression, for the people cannot share in a government which does not declare itself honestly, a government which deceives them, and so makes their participation impossible; And open statement, even an open statement of the greatest harshness, does not destroy the possibility of democracy and the peoples' rule: it is deception which does so.

Easier of course merely to be good to one's parents. They demand that one be happy. No one else demands that, but they cannot help demanding it, and one cannot always do it—. It is not only a burden, it not only doubles every failure, but it creates hopeless contradiction, confusion of values, abandonment of values——

The dream of many children, to be sorrowful and kind—. An attack on one's parents, a destruction of their hopes.

+ + +

Money—inherited money—looks to the past.
Every other family must look to the future.

The heiratic!

"Silence as an act of conflict"

Silence can be an act of combat. Stealth.

+ + +

A silly island, a silly island which will sit in the ocean
and wait for tourists

Whole and holy from the same root

all appetites inherent to life to be "cured"?
what we have is life
and its appetites

"therefore life will *always* be in the wrong"

+ + +

THE MEDICINAL: the mind becomes
human when it frees itself from the medicinal—

and even by expressing a doubt establishes a standard of "realness" as against the half way world of the common man in which nothing is quite real and which shelters him from fear. But what is real is, by its realness, frightening.

logic—the "logical" must—Why does it force one's hand? Words—something one learned as an infant, something the nurse uses—! they can be constructed like number into necessary truth.

Do we lack a transfinite syntax?
The vividness, the lucency of words

Any direction except back could be the way out. The idea, in Heidegger, that man may have to discard humanity in order to continue to live. One would have to go back to the "five year old questions" (Andy) to see why.[33]

everything you do from breakfast in bed to the perfume was an attempt NOT to live in the world. You think it is intelligence, can you not see that it is mindlessness!

Whatever God may be, he is not the hotel manager.

can you not give up this struggle *and live in the world?*

To think of no thing clearly, to perceive no object simply, is to avoid fear. But any experience of any art consists in not doing that.

—truly five-year old: to live because it is nice to have breakfast in bed.

Art can provide almost anything from wisdom to waltzes. But what art means to do is not to communicate experiences, but to communicate the "realness" of experience.

Stand on the edge of everything, afraid to enter it on equal terms. The judge in his wig may know a great deal—it is to be hoped he does—but he doesnt learn a damn thing

have to be babied—like a boy who wont enter—

And yet this is also the desire to live freely
Inside the rituals—

The thing is not to display the ego, but to use it—the instrument of perception

+ + +

You look at a statue and you see beyond it a statue, a form which would be perfect. Which you have never seen, and never will. Transcendence? perfect order?

The poem: correcting, one hears a line or a word as wrong, as against some idea of the good, the perfect—Correcting word by word, line by line, toward a concept which you hold, and have never experienced ?

The music of the poem does seem to be "out there," extant—
the sound towards which you are working
But why in the mind? where most clearly it is

Newton: the moment of tremendous excitement was the grasp of necessary truth. And the thought: I AM SAYING WORDS TO MYSELF BUT THOSE WORDS MUST REPRESENT THE TRUTH OF THINGS OUT THERE WHERE I HAVE NEVER BEEN AND CAN NEVER BE

The words must be true, the syntax must work! And words—something one has learned as an infant, something the nurse used—! They can be constructed like number into *necessary truth?*

Of the transcendental truth some things come—well, floating down in fragments like leaves of a tree—. As, numbers, which seem to act on necessary truth. *Do words? Do we lack a transfinite syntax?*

The Good (perfect) is necessary, not contingent, truth?

Number comes as if drifting down to us; It is there.
what does that mean to us?

One and zero: is and is not.

The Republic: how the human community should be ordered: which is Ethics

Rezi and I: the similarity of words. We have a degree of faith in the substantives which seem to have a one to one relationship to things out there

+ + +

the pulse
Of thought, which is the use of verse

"Gentle sadness" —just that I am aware there is not one to complain to, no one more fortunate than I.
to shout

They live freely—contingently—outside the rituals, and the commemorated events (the events of ritual)

the thing is not to display the ego in order to display a self, but to take it for granted, to use it as the instrument of perception. With all its contingency.

What we want is not an "idea" but the fact, the emotion of awareness, the emotion of consciousness.

—the emotion which leads toward knowledge—

See They Return—

The need
To be touched
By each other, stroked,
Pressed, lips, hands,
Genitals, the transports,
the extasies, loss
Of control—O the lonely
Particle forever exposed—
(I have even see people enjoying the rush hour, everybody push~~ing~~*es* ~~and being pushed~~ and they push back. And that is life. And it is good.
Or better—
And life will always be in the wrong?

<u>Gninnigeb eht ta nigeb</u>

—they have grasp of the concept of the self as subject, and they are overwhelmed. They cannot get their balance again—

that realization—some thing more than fifty thousand years ago, was an important moment in the history of man. But it is possible to get lost in it. The miracle, after all, is that there is something for us to stand on.[34]

Tho what terrors might we become
Companions of the natural,
The mineral orbits—? But the cities

+ + +

"The self as subject"

"everywhere, in reality, man is there, under cover.

"nature in her own fierce or solitary, unpiercable selfhood"

an unenterable—

he discerns it as inseparable for himself, from his emotion—

the self as a thing, among other things, with the distinction that it is experienced from the inside—the certainty that things are the future of the self—

you men may wish "to write poetry" At 55, my desires are more specific

possible   he knows something I do not. If he does, he will write it out, and be credited.

  nature, not hypocrite
Nor double
But ~~his~~ brother, closed,
Closed, less talented
Less vulnerable

"Quiet poems "—lacking, that is, the ~~sound of~~ blasting in Wales.

an event, caused to occur, need not throw rocks into the air

one cannot read the veritas etc as one reads: "jon groped his way down the stone steps and entered the dark, damp smelling cellar—It is the difference between reading and watching a movie—one need only read, and the thing is done to you—

(but what or which "you"? some slightly inauthentic "you")

To be rid of that (whole) crowd, for the effect of that crwod is to hamstring the whole cause by robbing it of its eriousness while pretending heartfelt sympathy' (Kirkegaard: the Present Moment)

they will write a ten page poem
with less effort and care than they will expend on
capculating how much money they will need for a tri½
to Philadelphia. --because that last will have to be
rightly, if they are going to 'see it differently' they
will have to 'see it differnetly' in fact. .

~~DIANE W Kirkegaard adresses one of his works to the reader thus: if he finds him --~~

~~I THINK A POEM SHOULD SEEM TO BE THE WORK OF A MAN WHO REALLY MEANS TO DRIVE A NAIL -- NOT TO STRIKE POSTURES OR TO SHOW OFF -- AND WHO KNOWS, HAS KNOWN FROM CHILDHOOD-- HOW A HAMMER SHOULD BE HANDLED.~~

I THINK A POEM SHOULD SEEM TO BE THE WORK OF A MAN
WHO REALLY MEANS TO DRIVE A NAIL -- NOT TO POSTURE
OR TO SHOW OFF -- AND WHO KNOWS, HAS KNOWN FROM
CHILDHOOD -- HOW A HAMMER SHOULD BE HANDLED.

DIANE W. Kirkegaard adress one of hos works to
the reader thus: if he finds him --
(Purity of heart, Preface, page 27

(The relationship of actuality)

"I — [illegible] you" — —
(it this may be exactly in
relationship of actuality

Daybook IV:I

Part 1 of the second "Pipe-Stem Daybook," papers bound by Oppen into a small makeshift book by means of pipe-stem cleaners (ca. 1966). Some of the pages are numbered in the upper right-hand corner, most likely by Mary Oppen (after George's death). There is no consecutive order. The first pages in the book (excised) are drafts of Oppen's introduction to a reading given by Diane Wakoski and William Bronk at the Guggenheim Museum in April 1966, suggesting a binding date somewhat thereafter. Also excised are drafts of poems published in *The Materials, This in Which,* and *Of Being Numerous,* drafts of published letters, and some illegible and ephemeral writings. In one instance (the middle of Oppen's second page), a bracketed ellipsis designates an illegible passage, ending with a colon, that precedes the transcribed passage "*relevant thought begins with the distrust of language*." Despite the illegibility, it is clear from the context that Oppen meant the sentence as a summation of sorts of the typed passage that immediately precedes it.

+ + +

We can say of the world that it is explained by God. And then we must say of God what we would have said of the world.
But all questions and all standards of relevant answers have been derived from our experience of the world.

It is possible to explain an engine. The flywheel actuated the push rods which open the correct valve at the proper moment which—etc; there is no difficulty, it can all be explained. But we are looking at the motor from outside. If there were nothing outside of this engine, and nothing before it nor after it, and no laws but those of the motor—if we could conceive of nothing beyond it or before it or after it——we would ask other questions.

We cannot see what is always present

+ + +

I take this to be a factual account:

The individual wakes ~~to~~ in the world. He wakes also to himself and to what he is—he discovers his arm. He seems to himself to be a consciousness which might well have been attached to a different person of different qualities—he discovers whether or not he is brave, whether or not he is clever—he had no opportunity to choose; all these things he found.[1]

this is the basic conception of being; he may marry or not, and he may succeed or not or he may be or not be admirable, but all this, all this of the novels, is superimposed on the basic awareness, the finding of things, the finding of the thing which can only at so great pain be accepted.

It is an insupportable situation for an animal to be human.

[. . .] *relevant thought begins with the distrust of language*.

As against the notion of an autonomous logic, of math, as "the man-made universe":
Fundamental ideas cannot be derived from each other.
"No entity can be conceived in complete abstraction from the system of the universe" (Whitehead in a different context): or, no entity, which is to say also no "idea" can be conceived as independent of the existence and the nature of the universe.[2]

We can say of the universe that it is explained by God. And thus we can say of God what we would have said about the universe.

+ + +

We ask ourselves (with passion) "How does it happen that anything exists?"

Ontology: a theory of Being

Ta onta: The the

Like Job we are answered
out of the whirl-wind.
There is no other answer
(Tho there is a voice)

+ + +

Like Job we are answered out of the whirl-wind

If, in the writing, the young poets will pay less attention to themselves, and more attention to the poem, they will discover marvelous places

i.e. to learn from the poem: to learn from the language

"Who if I cried would hear me"[3]

I doubt that the angels would listen to an ism.

+ + +

Bronk: that clarity & honesty can produce so piercing a music[4]

a poet who fits no school   whose work justifies no one's poetry but his own

Diane certainly among the strongest of the young poets.[5] There is in her poems a startling clarity of presence, uncompromising and courageous and exposed, unprotected, a startlingly clear and sustained voice. You will not fail to hear it—I promise that you will not.[6]

women blind
to the whole
notre pitie ce coeur—[7]
our pity is your heart—
which leads to all mud[8]

There remains compassion
it is hers   compassion

The marvelous
in space   no less sad
For being marvelous[9]

The pitfall of women poets: the prescription how to be good, how to be happy, how to be beautiful and nice also to be good: to lie and utter little gasps of pleasure when the world touches one—it is almost too seductive to speak of this bluntly. ~~They gasp with pleasure—~~ And better they wish to arrange things a little, they make suggestions—remembering their gasps—and everyone is infuriated.[10]

+ + +

Williams is wrong, merely wrong, whe~~re~~*n* he destroys ~~or does not achieve~~ the form of thought the form ~~of language~~, of perception, and ^*for*^ the sake of grace, of manner.

+ + +

Words stick in the mind
And refer to something that was
A moment ago or a long time past

And the poem, what does the poem refer to?

Is it perhaps abominable
In a time of atrocity
To write poems

Could one not stop[11]

I feel myself lit
Unconsumed ~~like~~ ^*as*^ a filament
So that time stops

Tho I give no light
But imagine light

An event which seems to be a part of an infinite series—
We are troubled by an infinite series, or the weight of ~~timelessness~~ unlimited time[12]

+ + +

"God". We choose our own words.

The reconciliation ^finally^ even to death in amor fati, the love of fate.[13] It is—even—an important love, like all love. Like all love expressed in events; it requires occurrences . . .

+ + +

I can only say it seems to me absurd to imagine a god who exists in transcendence and who speaks to man, or interferes in his affairs, or judges him. Life is, in any case, irrevocably committed to a world without a god; it postulates god only in that it <u>is</u> irrevocably committed

no deep penetration to their sex

"The Thinker," portrait of Louis N. Kenton. Which I called "the Intellectual"[14]

The women (Whistler's women) ~~raised~~ the tall women, raised on Alice in Wonderland and fairy tales emerge into an adulthood which contains only the rugs and the papered walls.[15]

And ordering servants——these young women!

The immense and helpless sea

Or the cloud, high and piled
Back upon itself
Voyaging alone

Deceives no one.

I write of things
Endless, endless,
Innumerable

"Man may not be treated as a means"
Oneself is also a man

Ethics therefore cannot consist in "doing good"?

No one has said it before . . . but perhaps an "important" poem
contains what could only have been said at that moment.
As Eliot's Wasteland.
"Wisdom" is never quite of the moment.

+ + +

Protected from despair by his youth. I do not mean animal high spirits, but that he is not all there is, there are men in front of him and his undertaking ~~and desire~~ is to get where they are. With no need for discovery ^*or invention*^, with no effort on his part, he has a place to go.[16]

But one cannot lead a life preparing for life, practicing for life, as for a football game. The "game" must finally have a purpose other than to succeed in it—

(Not perceived by sensory experience)
Being is nothing that we know, yet it is not nothing.
It actually is an intellectual conclusion.

I believe that Plato regards being as an essence; he is of no interest to me if it is so. I am concerned with ontological being, real being, not an ultimate abstraction

of all the things I doubt, I doubt most formal logic.

Ontological being—real being, including Linda's words—
not logical "being."

"the ruler rules . . . " is an absolutely impenetrable phrase to me. There is no such thing in the universe.

"Things happen"——of some force. We explain one event by another, but the force which causes things to happen is among the mysteries

A spontaneous or autonomous logic, if it exists, seems a subject for psychological *investigation*

+ + +

rime in bourg young people

There has been created a culture, a culture centering around Jazz, and perhaps largely the creation of the Negro, which is not a bourg possession, and young people are drawn into contact with classes ~~other~~ ^*not*^ their own—[17]

+ + +

Each decade a tap is opened
Which becomes the easiest thing to run out of.
It is exhilarating as running water.
This is an image

Of the fact
Of the thousands
Who in the name of originality
Are determined to write
As everyone else in that decade
Writes.

A ~~more public, or~~ less domestic art of originality would demand not so much that one write differently from his grandfather as that he should be distinguishable from his contemporaries—

At 18, 19, 20 the poet must find his contemporaries.
At 25, 26, 27 he must be distinguishable from them.
————this may be natural law.

+ + +

Well, there are moods. Why one writes—that's one thing. But whom is one addressing? and why? That bitch fame. That still more promiscuous bitch, neglect.[18]

+ + +

The groups:
what is wrong? most of these young people could never have written a line of poetry, could never have entered into that experience, if these groups did not exist, if the mode had not been established. And it is fine that they should, it can only be a gain— It is just my ill temper which bothers me, it is hard for me to contain my impatience when the platitudes of the moment are phrased and re-phrased around a room . . .[19]

+ + +

It does something with naturalism, or to naturalism, which has not before been done, and which has the most horrifying consequences. It transfers art to the outside world with a literalness not previously dreamt of, and in doing so shatters momentarily one's emotions concerning both art and the outside world. It produces a staggeringly dead world and a staggeringly dead art, and confronts one with his blank helplessness.[20]

Invent the word chordates and one has a thing to which one could be "loyal."

For the child, love means that he cannot despair while he believes in his parents. But for most adults love, tho it exists, is idle, non-operative. It is very much like a longing, a nostalgia

no one forgives failure—how can it be "forgiven"
When a man loses a leg, he is a one-legged man.

qualities

There seem to be two things most unpleasant: the characteristics ~~cre-ated by failure~~ which are a consequence of failure, and the qualities which are necessary to success.

At St. Paul's the little niggling voice behind me goes on and on

One could become fond of the gray days after such glories, seen from the little tea-shop

Good children, they will admit to their unhappiness—

"Forging a style," if one is sincere, is forging a syntax. We recognize it as a syntax when we recognize it as sincere.

I imagine a dog
Marooned like Crusoe[21]
And I think of that dog
As ephemeral
Yet I think of his life
As too long

I dislike most of all the theatrical ethic, the ethics of posture. The English gentleman, the fiery Latin, the Boulevardier or the hermit.

But can the survival of humanity, the continuation of humanity, be the highest good? Not very high then. For the meaning of the word "forever" is an impossibility

+ + +

Jung's point of departure from Freud:

That the psyche is always and only what it is. That it is also a single thing. The unconscious is ineluctably ~~present in~~ ^*a part of*^ the conscious^*ness*^ and moreover the conscious, even if it were possible to isolate it, cannot be taken as a perfect little machine which constructs a literal model of the universe.[22]

+ + +

To be rid of that (whole) crowd, for the effect of that crowd is to hamstring the whole cause by robbing it of its seriousness while pretending heartfelt sympathy" (Kierkegaard: the Present Moment)[23]

they will write a ten page poem with less effort and care than they will expend on capitulating how much money they will need for a trip to Philadelphia.—because that last will have to be right, if they are going to "see it differently" they will have to "see it differently" in fact.

DIANE W.[24] Kierkegaard addresses one of his works to the

~~I THINK A POEM SHOULD BE THE WORK OF A MAN WHO REALLY MEANS TO DRIVE A NAIL—NOT TO POSTURE OR TO SHOW OFF—AND WHO KNOWS, HAS KNOWN FROM CHILDHOOD—HOW A HAMMER SHOULD BE HANDLED.~~

I THINK THAT A POEM SHOULD BE THE WORK OF A MAN WHO REALLY MEANS TO DRIVE A NAIL—NOT TO POSTURE OR TO SHOW OFF—AND WHO KNOWS FROM CHILDHOOD—HOW A HAMMER SHOULD BE HANDLED.

DIANE W. Kierkegaard addresses one of his works to the reader thus: if he finds him—

(Purity of heart, Preface, page 27)[25]

(the relationships of actuality)

I— "like you"—
In this way he ^actually^ confronts the relationships of actuality

+ + +

"impossibly brilliant" young people, becoming a serious problem or a serious impossibility.

a forced growth. Mature minds, working at the top of their ability in the preparation of their lectures, exerting the great pressure they are capable of——the students encounter the wrong things at the wrong time, a matter of breaking the roots ~~I don't know if the sources are ever found again~~

Narrative, first section—

rapidly declares and ethic. And turns suddenly on the "or whether—"

(rejecting the social responsibility of poetry, but : if the poet writes clearly enuf to know, to know poetically what he is saying, whether he is not afraid to lie . . . He will find himself afraid to lie.[26]

—but——whether he is not in fact murderous.

certainly violent. The poem proceeds thru its experiences to the final "if we would rescue love." "if." it suggests no imperative, there's none in the poem. But if we would rescue Love—we will need clarity and scrupulousness. You will find it so. But it is a contingent ethic.[27]

(he discusses from "a taste" a prejudice, a mannerism—I can answer only be deliberate and, I hope forceful, non-sequitur)[28]

To stand alone is not my problem. That is easily done.
Too easily.

"When all is called by its own name, yet there is nothing said"
S Kierkegaard.[29]

The moral issue: simply whether or not one is willing to know what he has said—or whether or not he is willing to say anything.

Thru Pound and Williams the young men have found a breaking of conventional forms, a releasing of speech which in the end will leave them outside the shelter of cliche. And that will lead them eventually to a reappraisal of Stevens and Eliot of the Quartets. For Pound and Williams are without <u>*intellectual*</u> *interest.*

+ + +

There is also the question whether it is any longer possible for an artist or poet to be seen or heard unless he is part of a group. If a single artist, not a group, had produced the devastating art which has found the name Pop—Would he have been recognized at all? Perhaps there are too many claims on attention and response, perhaps no one is willing to take the pains to understand a poet or an artist or in fact to give him ~~any~~ ^*enuf*^ attention ~~at all~~ ^*to know what he is saying*^ without the assurance that one is thereby understanding an entire group at a single blow—. I think this is the reason for the extraordinarily delayed recognition of precisely those men whose work has most value. I raise this point because Bronk surely must be heard as himself, and not as a group.

+ + +

Creeley is turning over and over in his poems the question whether two people can be faithful to each other. Well, as to that: yes, they can.

The scholastic philosophers: their systems would seem as permanent as the assumption—they would say the faith—on which they are based; the assumption of infinite being, which would seem a necessary fact provided one recognize the meaning of infinite as non-finite—a negative theology.

We would have to know the force which causes a thing to be—

+ + +

They are scarcely seen, they are felt rather than seen, there is the greatest difficulty in making them felt by those who do not of themselves perceive them . . . and to judge rightly and justly of when they are perceived . . .

for the expression of it is beyond all men and only a few can feel it

Pascal[30]

It is a question not likely to be answered. It cuts under theology also: at least, theology.

How it happens that there is such a thing as actuality

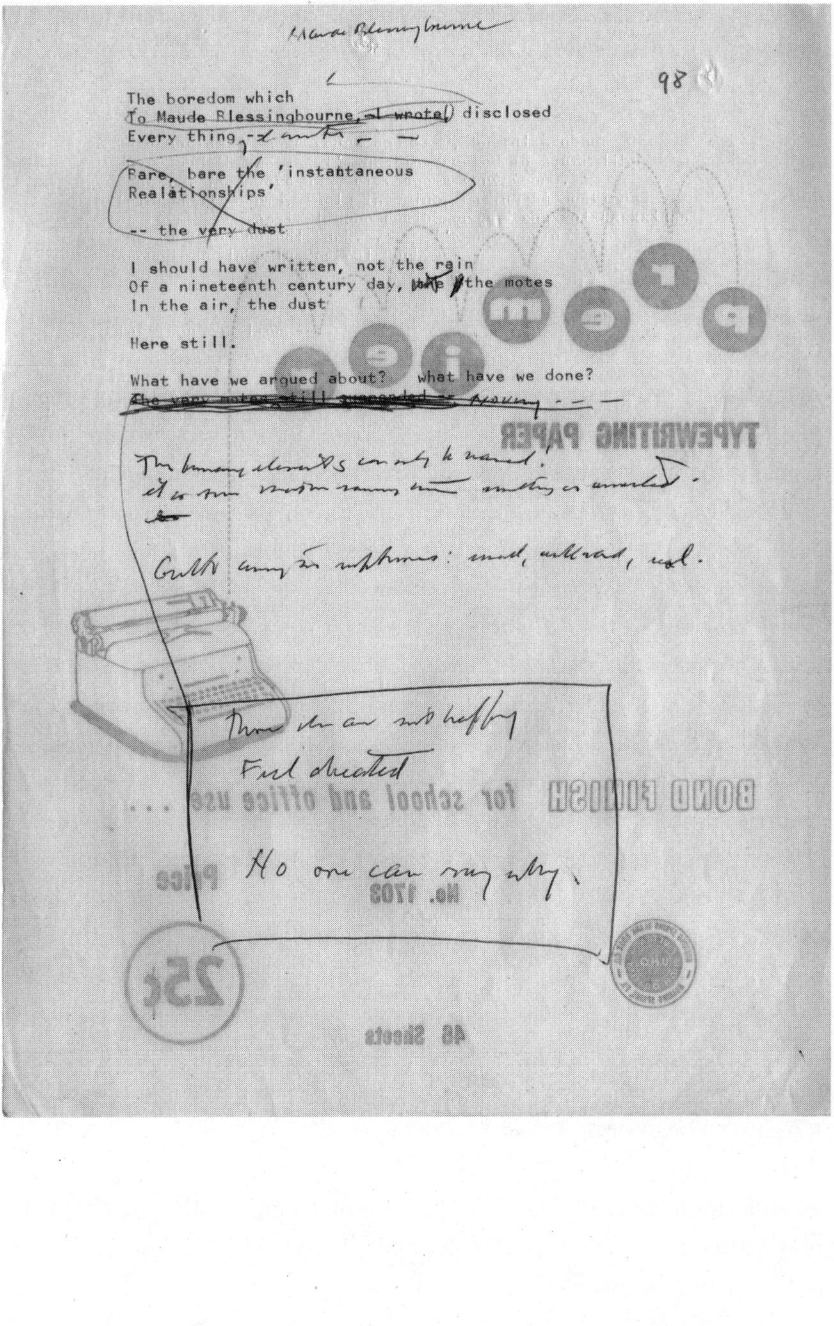
Maude Blessingbourne

98

The boredom which
~~To Maude Blessingbourne, I wrote)~~ disclosed
Every thing, [illegible] — —

~~Rare, bare the 'instantaneous~~
~~Realationships'~~

~~-- the very dust~~

I should have written, not the rain
Of a nineteenth century day, ~~the~~ the motes
In the air, the dust

Here still.

What have we argued about? what have we done?
~~The very motes still suspended or~~ moving . — —

The boring elements can only be named.
[illegible]
~~[illegible]~~

[illegible]

Those who are not happy
Feel cheated

No one can say why.

Daybook IV:II

Part 2 of "Stapled Daybook II." Excisions include poem drafts, drafts of letters, ephemeral and illegible writings.

+ + +

There are risks one must take if he wishes to write poetry—

They are very considerable risks. The risk of exposing his mere self, to begin with, that is the first hurdle, and most never surmount it. And the risk of facing what he knows, what, really, we all know, of parting with ~~platitudes~~ ^*new statements*^, including those of the avant-garde of the moment. Which is a serious risk. But the risk of shocking someone? There is no such risk. There is no meaning in the concept of avant garde today—

There are the groups—. I suppose one has a right, it provided a life and it provides print—Yet I tend to believe very strongly that what one must do is go off by himself, to make his own life, to guarantee himself as a person, first of all———And write from there. He's likely to be very old before he's printed if he does that————But I think there is no other way to write real poetry.

and ^*surely*^ there is no other experiment worth making——

On those whose work is derivative:

To shift one's style, shift one's eyes. Look at something else. Look until one begins to hear, to hear its form and size ^*the shape it would fill*^: it imposes itself.

or, if ~~one's interests~~ ones life and concerns coincide ineluctably with those of another poet——— Look further.

~~then~~ It becomes hard to ~~do~~ ^*write*^, of course; hard to find a form, a sound, a notation, a way to say it all! Well, I think, simply, it isnt as easy. But that is poetry, that is the use of poetry. *And the only experiment worth making.*

easy to set up the experiment: look at a flower in a crannied wall—if there's one to be found, or such as one can find—and look further, with all we know, with all that has happened—

+ + +

"The Fall"—obviously the sin of pride. Man's tragedy is his awareness of good and evil—it seems a more accurate statement of the causes of human happiness and of the evolution of man than the Buddhist. The tree "desires" to reach the sunlight. There does not seem any justification for thinking of it as "unhappy" if it is frustrated, it merely acts as it is constituted to act and continues to try.

but the Christian concept seems hopelessly irreconcilable with the beneficent God, of course. The question of free will aside: if the will is free, it acts according to its nature, which was created———[1]

(nothing in an individual which can determine what the will shall will; if there were, we would call it the will. Therefore there can be nothing that we do not call the will which can determine what we shall want.

The will can be divided, it can will two things. As a child, do you want to see a movie or do you want to be home to meet Daddy, and he is more likely to say "both." His answer is perfectly accurate, he does not possess the word "prefer" which meant to want two things but to want one thing more than the other— It can of course be difficult to choose between two things that one wants———but this is not really "struggling with one's will" Only the will can struggle with the will

+ + +

Not the end of American history at this moment. For this reason:

I believe that we lack a practicable means of recalling a president, even in the case of a president who is deranged, and I do not know therefore if Johnson can be stopped. If he cannot be stopped, we are surely going to attack China. It is true that Russia cannot permit an American occupation of China, but Russia will not be opposed to a considerable weakening of China, and she will certainly not mind if the US loses two or three armies in China. And this is what will happen. We will not succeed in occupying China, therefore there is no reason to suppose that the U S and Russia will be destroyed.

What will happen, if Johnson is not restrained or removed, is that several tens of millions of Chinese will be killed, and several millions of American young men. I do not know if these young men, or their wives and parents will agree to give their lives to the CIA game; perhaps they will, perhaps they are very bored. If they are that bored, I don't suppose that this country or its people will survive long.[2]

+ + +

I cannot face the war. Diane wrote something about acceptance, the ability to accept.[3] I cannot accept. And it is true that to be absolutely unable to accept ^*something that happens, things that happen*^ is to be destroyed

I am not able to listen to people, I can not listen or talk to people—I feel as if the thing had ended, or become meaningless

Socrates, and the goal of "virtue . . .
The "goal" is to know. If man as a society, as whenever an individual man despairs once and for all of the possibility of "knowing," there remains the sentiment of compassion, a sort of negative ethic, but no other ethic, no other control of one's conduct.

There are objective forms which have meaning for us, and which we live among, which we cannot escape, and when we see them clearly we ^*understand*^ our true natures.

+ + +

Johnson's war: a decisive act. it will guarantee that fully half the people in the world will remain communists—devoted communists—for a long time to come.

+ + +

Perhaps it has no form, we move thru it
"An indeterminate medium . . .
Empty of value" (Brumbaugh)[4]

Perhaps it will end.

A life worth living is not easy, because we want to know; not to read, but to know. As Lear's life, Finally, was about,

worth living.

Antin's objection to the "closed form": If one reaches a conclusion, a place to stand, let him say so.[5] As Rezi's "a girder, still itself among the rubble." He has a right, I think, to stand on that.[6]

Antin enjoying the escape from form which he still feels—well, as an escape.

+ + +

I can't imagine myself that there is a spontaneous or autonomous logic. It seems to me that meaning is found in the experience of phenomena. It is impossible to assume that the world of things could be proved if one had not experienced it—we would not possess the word "is" ^which means logic & thought, including mathematical logic^ *if ~~we did not exist.~~*
we had not experienced existing

The whole [ ], including the desire to live. It is a [ ], but a strange one—a [ ] which has lived

+ + +

The creating <u>now</u> "at the roots of the grass."[7] One ant avoids another and that is now—— Not to confuse it thru some specious drama the event may have for oneself. It rains, and a thirsty man is saved in the desert. But what happened was that ~~simply~~ it rained. And that was now.

One ant avoids another
And that is now

The roots in the grass.
It rains, and a thirsty man
is saved. But what happens
is that the rain falls.
And that was now.

One ant
avoids another, and that ~~was~~ ^becomes^ now.

It rains, and extinguishes a fire, and
a man is saved. But what happened
was that it rained. And that was now.

+ + +

On the Prosody and Numbers of X

The peculiar attributes of words is that they spring spontaneously in the mind, they flow continuously in the mind. They provide, if not hope, at least opacity.

And a peculiar thing happens: one ceases to be sure who is speaking, one is, as they say, conversing with himself. And of course there is safety in numbers.

To regard possession of the world by—statistics?
Or in statistics we lose even ourselves?
We learn from statistics that our feelings are irrelevant?

+ + +

Unwilling to construct a systematic aesthetics, still must add that we "engender in beauty." I don't want to try here to explore that. Would we discover our faith in Goodness, the Good, or simply the emotional component? Possible to discuss "prosody" at this level. But How To Write A Poem ended, as it should, with the letters   O   K   .

This is my post-post-graduate present.[8]

+ + +

The boredom which
To Maude Blessingbourne, ~~I wrote!~~, disclosed
Every thing, ^*I wrote*^—

~~Bare, bare the "instantaneous~~
~~Relationships"~~

~~—the very dust~~

I should have written, not the rain
Of a nineteenth century day, ^*but*^ the motes
In the air, the dust

Here still.[9]

What have we argued about?   what have we done?
~~The very motes, still suspended~~ *No very*

The human elements can only be named!
it is from [   ] *naming that something is invented.*

Guilt among the morphemes: sound, awkward, real.

Tho we are not happy
Feel cheated

No one can say why.

The human elements can only be named!

+ + +

Pete saying—some years ago—O, he talks about death and things—I'm not interested in stuff like that . . . And Dave at thirty seems very young, talks about poems, including mine, making suggestions as to my form as if I were rowing around the lake in Central Park . . . I'm not rowing around the lake in Central Park—[10]

Lay it on the line—

+ + +

Duncan: not sincerely "a Jungian," but he resembles Jung in that he believes in the existence of an extraordinary number of things, many of which have capitals which are meant to give them a significance which I am unable to imagine.

<u>*"Artist of the [ ]"*</u>

the use of adjectives: I've said that I believe in the "things" represented by nouns. I think I may seem a miracle of the pious—if not sentimental—credulity to future generations. ~~But~~ It is an act of faith. And I rely therefore on the nouns. Where I am speaking of subjective reaction, I use adjectives freely enough—

In the garden
Outside, and so beautiful![11]

"beautiful" is an adjective.
Since I don't use many, I don't need a very fancy one.

+ + +

Giotto among the sumptuous: small, awkward, Rezi[12]

Whatever does not itself acknowledge that it is supposed to serve a purpose—is unspeakable mystery.
The "god" is Atlas, not the turtle or rock

+ + +

consciousness reaches finally an awareness of the circumstances of its own origin, a knowledge more terrifying than the knowledge of death

We know the circumstances
Of our origin, more disturbing
Than the knowledge of death.

"And mourn Dido dead because she killed herself for love" [ ][13]

BRONK an intellectual insight which becomes an emotional force thru the recognition of its limits, the recognition of its failures—("the center of things")[14]

it seems to me that such poems as The Feeling, To the Virgin, Not My Lonliness, but Ours, etc must become a permanent part of literature—I do not see how they can be forgotten.

DIANE an amazing poetry, absolutely her own, absolutely lucid.[15] The poems seem to me surely among the best poems of her generation.

"In these explanations it is presumed that an experiencing subject is one occasion of a sensitive reaction to an actual world" Whitehead, Process and Reality, page 24

I don't know—one would answer Steve—what a non-experienced world would be. I'm not convinced that it is possible to understand the question. But I would say with Whitehead that entities actually involve each other by their prehension of each other.

And that science has been proceeding for some time thru a process of division, the division of the object into atoms, etc. The process of division has acquired great prestige, and one is likely to refuse to abstract from the molecule to the bar of steel. And yet there is no question that we experience the bar of steel.

one is likely to forget that the bar of steel is an abstraction

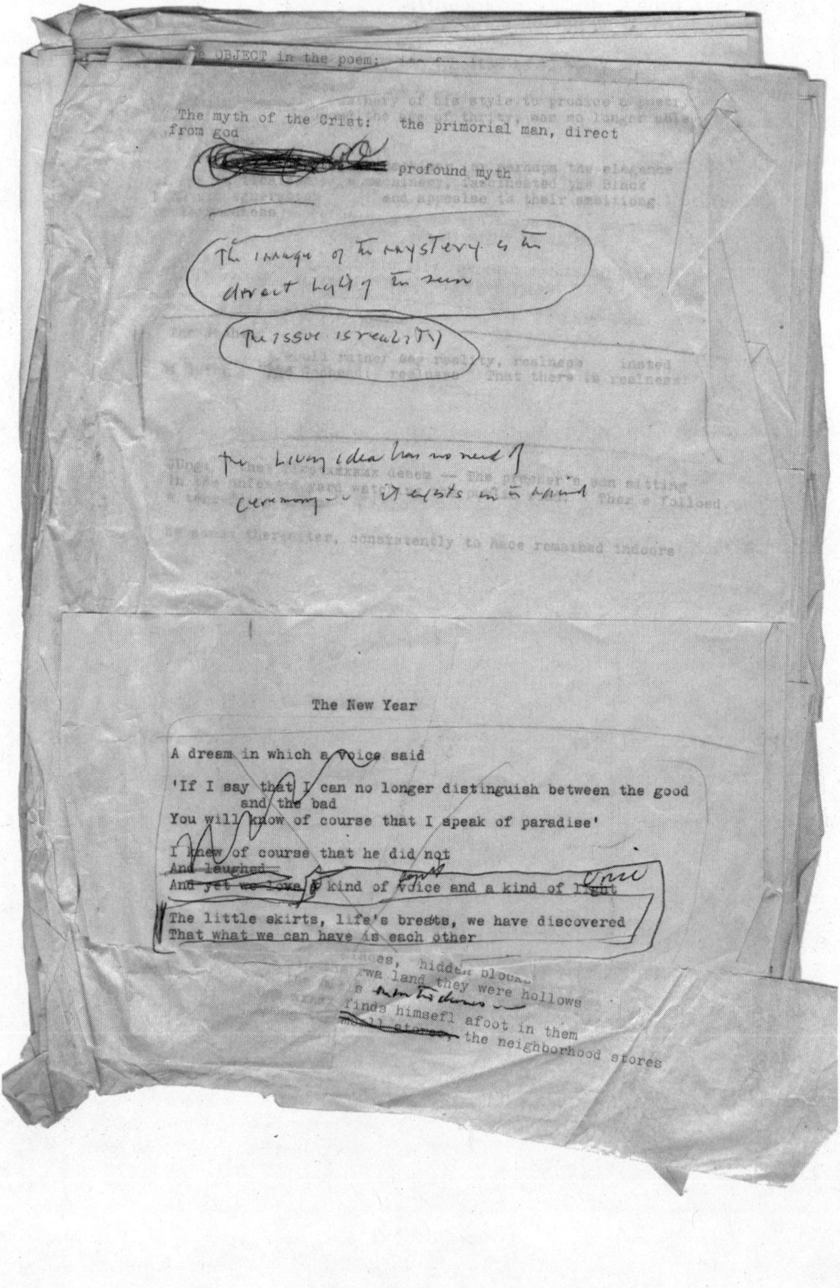

OBJECT in the poem;

The myth of the Crist: the primorial man, direct from god

profound myth

The image of the mystery is the direct light of the sun

The issue is reality

would rather see reality, realness insted

realness That there is realness

The living idea has no need of ceremony — it exists in the hand

The New Year

A dream in which a voice said

'If I say that I can no longer distinguish between the good
and the bad
You will know of course that I speak of paradise'

I knew of course that he did not
~~And laughed~~
~~And yet we love~~ a kind of voice and a kind of light

The little skirts, life's breats, we have discovered
That what we can have is each other

ces, hidden blocks
wa land they were hollows
finds himsefl afoot in them
~~small stores,~~ the neighborhood stores

Daybook V

The pages of Daybook V were bound tightly at the left by glue or paste. Small strips of paper containing fragments of Oppen's writing of various length are pasted over many of the sheets. The bound document as a whole appears in the archive under the varying titles "Christ Note-Stack" and "New Year: Pasted Daybook," presumably due to the content of the first page, as well the theological tropes (much of them based on Oppen's reading of Carl Jung's work, especially *Memories, Dreams, Reflections*) that run throughout the work. I have changed the title, however, for the following reasons: (1) the figure of Christ and/or the reference to the "New Year" are ultimately no more central to Oppen's reflections in these writings than are any number of other figures, tropes, or motifs (the experience of war, the epistemological validity of poetry, more generally theological musings, etc.); (2) neither "note-stack" nor "daybook" fully conveys the complex manner in which Oppen worked on the writings here, which involved his cutting of phrases from one sheet of paper and pasting them on another, often to depth of several leaves (a practice which he uses often in revising or, perhaps better, *reconstructing* his poetry). Therefore, in my title, I have borrowed the term *palimtext* from Michael Davidson, which has the benefit of more accurately describing the "palimtextual" (cut-and-paste, pseudocollage) nature of the document.[1] I have added the subtitle "Of the Needle's Eye" based on Oppen's inclusion of four variously annotated and epigraphed "title pages" of his first draft of what would later become *Seascape: Needle's Eye*. The benefit of this title lies not solely in a thematic linking of these materials to the composition of that volume (a link that, given the nature of Oppen's materials, is tenuous), but also in that it dates these writings as having been produced roughly between 1969 and 1972, the primary years during which Oppen was working on that manuscript.

Due to the uniquely spatial nature of this "palimtext," I have retained all of Oppen's hard returns, rather than justifying prose passages in accordance with the textual apparatus.

+ + +

OBJECT in the poem: its function is to burst[2]

The myth of the Christ: the primordial man, direct from god

profound myth

The image of the mystery is the direct light of the sun

The issue is reality

the living idea has no need of ceremony—it exists in the mind

---

The New Year

~~A dream in which a voice said~~

~~"If I say that I can no longer distinguish between the good~~
~~and the bad~~
~~You will know of course that I speak of paradise"~~

~~I knew of course that he did not~~
~~And laughed~~
~~And yet we love~~ a kind of ^*light*^ voice and a kind of ~~light~~ ^*voice*^
The little skirts, life's breasts, we have discovered
That what we can have is each other

"hidden" places, hidden blocks
——in the raw land they were hollows
"In the hills ^in the distance—^
One finds himself afoot in them
Among ~~the small stores~~, the neighborhood stores

+++

OBJECT in the poem: its function is to burst

historical religion

[ ] machinery of his style to produce a poetry
th[ ]beyond the age of thirty, was no longer able
to pr [

][3] the rumbling of machinery, or perhaps the elegance of the implication of a machinery, fascinated the Black mountain generation and appeals to their ambitions of learnedness[4]

The Godhead

I would rather say reality, realness instead
of Being The Godhead: realness That there is realness

Jung: that first dream—the preacher's son sitting in the unfenced yard watching the public road. There followed a terrifying dream

he seems thereafter, consistently to have remained indoors[5]

(the universe))

~~withdraws~~ ^*withdrew*^, and will not live, but holds
its strength, its height, its distances

"hidden" places, hidden blocks
——in the raw land they were hollows
"In the hills ^*in the distance—*^
One finds himself afoot in them
Among ~~the small stores~~, the neighborhood stores

+ + +

OBJECT in the poem: its function is to burst

" . . . It was the first time I had ever seen a black woman look at a Black man with unmixed admiration"[6]

~~How can one argue about this?~~ ^*Argue?*^ One can argue about anything else that he wants to, but he cannot argue about this

And if a man even once in his life has said something like ~~this~~ ^*it*^, if you betray him you must cut your throat

((meaning: a man or a woman has a right to be loved,
If he cannot ~~be,~~ he will try to destroy the world

and you cannot betray him. Or if you do, you
  must cut your throat

+ + +

"hidden places" in the town hidden blocks—
in the raw land they were hollows ~~in the~~
 In the hills or among the dunes
One finds himself afoot in these blocks
Among the neighborhood stores

One finds himself afoot among the stores
among hidden hills and dunes
illuminated

What is in the center is the center, not a god.
The god if he is placed there obliterates the center and demands, instead, a frame c——[7]
XXXXX

There is no birth in
Jung: no act of birth.
He disregards it.

it seems that in the center of the universe, if there is a center, can be only one's own peace, one's own wholeness.

---

astrology: I would not tend to ~~find meaning~~ attach meaning to merely circular time

+ + +

The historical religion: the religion of salvation

The force of life ~~to be~~ all-powerful in the resurrection and the "kingdom" *No "dead matter"*
does this explain "this is my body, this is my blood" ie: all substance, existence, ~~to be life~~ will be life

It seems true that this is the last age we have come as far as is possible The force of life beyond this age will be all-powerful, or it will be vanquished utterly Vanquished by its limitation, by having reached its own limits, by boredom

Was it a mystery, a dream
of lying day after day on one's belly in fear
on the hard ground
under the rifle-fire[8]

He took the substance nearest at hand. It was a dinner: he took a piece of bread and a glass of wine. He said this is my body and my blood.
the world is the body of God. One must say this, or one must say (in these terms) that it is the devil

(I neither like nor dislike "these terms" That are available. And I am suspicious of speaking Chinese or Japanese or Hindu: we are likely to deceive ourselves through mere exoticism)

+ + +

Orphic: the trees ~~fell~~ ^*moved*^ when he sang, the boat
moved down the ways. he sang to the birds
and reach the dead

It is the "sympathy" of the poet with the world

Empedocles: (Orphic school):
I was once a boy and a girl, a bush and a
mute fish rising from the depth of the sea

Mute fish

Drowning ~~in his own depths in the depths of the sea~~[9]

Wordsworth's proof of immortality: the spirit of the very young child the spirit born in him[10]

or: Katharsis, the gradual ascent of the soul to the world of being

The covenant is: there shall be people[11]

"Immortality"; as the fame of a man in his city-state

the poet's "contact with his own destiny"

The music is the core of the poem's meaning

"Since there are too many people, we must be animals or
Buddhas"   Snyder[12]

One's own song, as the Indian

The survivor of the world of matter

"and if there should be a god he is with you in the ringing of the bells
and fragrance of the incense, but not in Stalingrad"
letters from Stalingrad[13]

a poetry adequate
more adequate if it stood alone? if there
had been no literature behind it? or less literature?

to avoid, at least, the readings, the reviews, the world of "comparative
literature"

archangel of the Moments
(*Moments)*

+ + +

The OBJECT in the poem: its function is to burst
the boundaries of the poem

Nature shuddered and spoke in fear

What manner of new mystery is this?
The invisible is seen and is not ashamed

Maleto of Sardis[14]

This is Grandpa's house, and it's mine
This is Grandpa's suit, and it's mine.
This is Grandpa's ~~face~~! And it's
mine!

Wyeth: who discloses
"the blatant mystery ~~(Mary)~~
of objects" (Mary)[15]

Speaking candidly (of the Needle Eye)
it begins to reach heaven—
To glimpse heaven

But there were Three crosses

+ + +

David:

acknowledge the emotions   Acknowledge the emotions or you'll die   A machine doesnt think for its own purposes at all: what does think for its own purposes is not a machine[16]

Earth, my sister
Little ~~spinning~~ ^dancing^ sister
Little lonely sister

Earth   my sister
~~Little~~ Dancing sister
Little lonely sister

Earth, my sister *dancing sister* *little lonely sister* *my matter*[17]

+ + +

THEY HAVE REDISCOVERED ARCHAIC
TRADITIONS   ARCHAIC INSIGHTS
AND THOUGHTS   THEY HAVE ADDED NOTHING TO
THEM   THE
REDISCOVERED WORDS REMAIN WHAT THEY WERE
THEY VALUE ORTHODOXY!!!   they blame themselves that
the ancient
words will not remain perfectly what they were

first   the void: whole-heartedly?
They cannot   they will not   and   one doesnt dare
wish that they could   *But in philosophizing human uni-verse*[18]

---

among the great moments of history   cannot predict its
outcome

---

epic fidelity   fidelity to life

answer to the "feminine art" of the left "what books
did you read   what books were important"   and then one
finds the Plato-Stalin-Mao attitude: the poets lie too
much   i.e. the poets move on, therefore they lie

the self-importance of the artists

Snyder   he likes mountains   Which is genuine And in the mountains he likes to remember the tremendous adventure of the monasteries and someone saying something like "the universe is in the shape of a conch-shell"

it isn't unattractive

needle's eye   center   center of the mandala   shadowless
water, shadow of water ——— Void   But is perhaps also
the center (tho it is a void) of individuation

Tribal   —a nostalgia   I feel it too   perhaps

they may believe, like Jung, that there is no linear
evolution, but only a circumambulation of the self

"for methe self   " (the center of mandala) is
the ultimate"   and adds: perhaps someone else
knows more[19]

a man is a man   Limit to the amount of fooling   Take
one or leave them all

+ + +

the evolutionary hypothesis is a reversal of the natural laws of
chance   a destruction, a violation of the "natural" order

the proliferation and dominance of man carries forward this "un-natural" order

the return to nature is not, then, what is going to occur
Nature has . . . . ?

Nature

"oneness" "harmony": a man falls head down into a crevasse in the ice He is wedged tight, ~~unable to move his arms~~

He is alone: no-one knows he is there[20]

---

fields of the mock-sage

---

take any road Don't keep your eyes on the map

or on your feet. If the road is pre-occupying, SWERVE OFF
Wander Swerve

To the tribes: of course nothing has any value whatever but love

who do you love and where is she

We are not returning to nature We are playing out the drama of free will Having come so far, we must

the communities

also playing out that drama they have wanted to know if they are free even of the culture

^*Even the "revolution," the return to Nature,*
is an exercise in free will Not in piety

---

we must trust our own will or trust the instincts of rulers

—

extended youth   a major factor   The traditional family cannot shelter children into their twenties   and even beyond

—as for "the revolution": the traditional family has already collapsed

But it is among the past
No remnants of history. I cant
predict its outcome

+ + +

"loss of identity   loss of the ego   But in fact being
accepted into a group ^*he*^ thinks with exultation   ME
ME   I'M being accepted into the group!

It is difficult if not impossible
to feel the validity of [   ] or
[   ] in any <u>*picture*</u>
of the world

the three Jungion visions: it occurs to me that
I got told:

yes, it's a woman down there And yes, very beautiful ~~to~~
~~me~~   and then: it is, however, a dry stream-bed
[   ]   *any stream-bed of mother*
((also got told about the woman "impaled,"   slightly
painful, disconnected, slightly ridiculous

---

what is seen in the window is "realism"   what is seen
in the mirror is beauty

But beauty does appear to reflect
~~*to shine: to reflect*~~ to shimmer
the world: to reflect!

ISSUING FROM THE CAVE   HE SAW THE SUN AND
RECOGNIZED
~~IN THE SUN HIS~~ NATIVE LAND.   And saw it was deserted

+ + +

I think the world is very big, and a piece of canvas
is very small

The road where no one has walked
Why is the road here?
~~Is it possible no one has walked it?~~
Something haunts the road   ~~Emptyness?~~
~~Emptyness haunts~~
Why is the road here

If "God" means the unknown whole of which one is a part, then God
is the word to use.   And certainly one may speak of love.
One cannot adequately ^*speak*^ one's love.

the existence of the world means the possibility of happiness
(That without which I could not be myself)

"Follow me"   to the agony?   court agony for the children also?

——

those who chase after the audience are bound to be behind. they may not feel loneliness   they must surely find their position undignified

or ! the ego attacked by incomprehensible surroundings

It seems clear that I inherit my father's life—therefore the lives of all ancestors   It can be said that I am my ancestors   but not that I was my ancestors   Or will be my descendents   The product of a process: I WAS not until I was created by that process

---

eye of the needle   image
of the horizon   destitute metal   what [
] but or although in a world's picture[21]

"freely tumultuous" as the tremendous volume of the music takes over obscured by their long hair they seem to be mourning

---

+ + +

---

eye of the needle image
of the horizon destitute metal who ~~will~~
~~say~~ but or although in a world's picture

+ + +

"but's and although's are too weak to put into
a cosmic picture too weak to put even into a
picture of one's awareness

+ + +

as periods draw to a close, the arts spin out a
world of their own, incredibly silly, ~~incredibly
limited, far more limited than the general vision~~

*You would like a few asian words in the text.
And then, because you had not understood
it, you would feel that you had understood
it.*

+ + +

The distinction being made between thought and emotion argues a lack of both thought and emotion—or at least extreme shallowness of thought and emotion

emotion without thought is "sensation"
thought which is mere puzzle-solving may be without emotion

tho it is difficult to see how thought can be motivated, or
therefore can occur without emotion

Indian men and Indian women mustered all the courage each could
among the dangers of humiliation, affliction, enslavement, *and*
So do we

> *Emotion put in Motion*
> *Nothing else does except physical force.*

> *If, as in the Winter light, the response is joy, or*
> *if love should simply come to an end—?*

+ + +

Surely that vision said: the way to the unconscious
is thru the feminine thru the pool and the river
of the feminine to the interior —— *(But the first vision—the impaled female?)*

And I had called the new book: of the needle's eye
And then the fortune cookie: If you have lost your
needle etc I had even asked myself: What
does a needle symbolize? Phallus, I asked? but
obviously a needle is a symbol of femininity!!

And I had overlooked this despite the fact that I had
hesitated to quote the sentence on the fly leaf <u>because</u>
the "needle" seemed inappropriate—being a feminine
possession

ANIMA MUNDI—the spirit of the world, which is the life Spirit

The basic concept is the life spirit as anima mundi

Gold morning, the red hinge
Spans a part of it

I build with the materials at hand, or
enter combat with David's sling-shot

The Simple Life

Thank God for the hungry
We would have said had we been honest
Thank God for the exhausted planet
Now, thank god for the enemy
God grant that we do not solve this matter

Well— ~~*It looks rather like eternity*~~
(a small boat at sea)
The sea from a small boat looks rather
like eternity it is a [ ]
(the modern) God becomes lighter & farther
as ration disappears

+ + +

The feminine: They move within, touching everything,
seeing everything, destroying nothing ^*nothing to destroy*^ ~~. As I can not do~~
But they never break out!

The music of a poem
is wave after wave
of meaning. The wave
must be perfect. Each
wave as perfect as the wave of pitch,
perfect as the wave of rhythm

Hidden from the image of the needle
image of the [ ], *has died* [
] *pounds again & again*
on the one ~~*nail*~~
~~*post*~~
spike
Drill[22]

a hidden moral of it is that God ^[ ] *or little mammal haunts human justice*^ *would like man to grasp the Truth*

+ + +

Party on Shipboard:
like the waves, the people, appearing as

individual, are accidents of the single
mass, a single body

—and a Party on ~~Shipboard~~
shipboard is a farewell[23]

Pools of blood , the skins pierced
And the count of them lost,
Uncountable
People dying alone

The rules are rather thoroughly proven— It is certainly possible that the rules are sometimes violated

---

Sitting in the work room, over the typewriter or the desk there comes suddenly the sense of being absolutely alone It is then that the line arrives

Francis Ponge who says: "Every desire to flee weights me with a new link to the chain"[24]

Unredeemed

+ + +

Perhaps whenever one makes a choice he leaves another himself ~~leaves not~~ within him, ^*some other self*^ cut off from the major muscles

and isolated, therefore, from the world   from the effective
and affective world—

I still feel that "proletarian"——
The pure maker?   the banger, the pounder?   one of the
men?—struggling around in my innards

I have fallen from the tree

I am not dead

I do not know what will become of me

Twenty-Six Fragments

Twenty-Six Fragments

Entitled by archivists, in collaboration with Mary Oppen, "The Last Words of George Oppen," "Twenty-Six Fragments" consists of a series of notes scrawled by Oppen on envelopes and other small pieces of paper found, after his death, on or near his desk or pasted to the wall of his study. Some of the fragments were numbered by Oppen, others were not. One fragment (12) was found written in pencil on Oppen's wall. Although these are among the last writings Oppen is known to have produced, there is no way of determining the exact date of composition, nor does the content suggest any conscious desire on Oppen's part to mark them as conclusive or final. I have therefore adopted a less misleading title.

The documents appear in two files in Oppen's archive. The first is Mary Oppen's numbered and sequenced transcription, contained in a small wire-bound notebook. The second consists of the original documents, composed in Oppen's hand. Appearing here is a text based on Mary Oppen's transcription, with the following revisions: (1) I have added the last line in fragment 6, which appears in George Oppen's file but not in Mary Oppen's. (2) I have added the first line in fragment 12, which appears in George Oppen's file but not in Mary Oppen's. It is possible that the line was composed in a hand other than Oppen's (it is written either in crayon or in bold marker), but this is not definite. It is, however, certain that Oppen's line follows from the first, and thus I have let it stand. (3) I have changed fragments 17a and 17b, numbered as such in Mary Oppen's transcription, to fragments 17b and 17c, respectively. Fragment 17a as it appears here is crossed out in Mary Oppen's transcription, and is numbered 17 out of sequence. (4) George Oppen's "live" replaces Mary Oppen's "look" in fragment 19a. (5) I have added fragment 22, which did not exist in Mary Oppen's transcription, and which exists unnumbered among the other papers in George Oppen's file. There is no fragment 22 in Mary Oppen's file. (6) I have added boxes to indicate text that is circled in George Oppen's file. With the exception of fragment 8, Mary Oppen's transcription does not indicate circled text.

+ + +

1.
Music, that marvel
trying to exist
out of this forest to come forth

2.
I find I am forgetting

all the spoken   of
and the numbers   (i.e.
how to form them

---

also the numbers

3.
We don't really know what
Reality is made of

4.
In the play, the actors cry out
But in the poem the words
themselves cry out

5.
Being with Mary: it has
been almost too wonderful
it is hard to believe

6.
I am not sure whether or not
I would like to live altogether
In the forest of poetry
Its mystery and its clarity

7.
I think I have written what I
set out to say—I need
not now turn to narrative

I have told not narrative, but
ourselves—no narrative but ourselves

6. I am not sure whether or not
I would like to ~~have~~ live altogether
in the forest of poetry:

It's airy

7. I think I have written what I
set out to say... I need
not now turn to narrative

I have told not narrative, but
ourselves -- no narrative but
ourselves

8. I would speak of the world:
I would speak for the world

(Crossed out)
M.O.

~~9. Poetry must be~~
15. We are entering a new era
and nothing will be the same in the storm
STORM

(Written while that storm was
blowing

Post Post Modern

9. "Clarity" means, among
other things, to know
how the words come to meaning.—

To *experience* how the
words come to meaning

A note to Pound in heaven:

Only one mistake, Ezra!
You should have talked
to women

Poetry ~~[illegible]~~ at least
as powerful as music, but
I am not sure that
it is possible

10. People visit, and I am
shaken

11. Our little bird: I
feel all my
boyhood in
him

12 (in pencil on wall) The World is
half magic

8.

I would speak of the world: I would speak for the world

9.
~~Poetry must be~~

Clarity means, among
other things, to know
how the words come to
meaning

to <u>experience</u> how the
    words come to meaning

A note to Pound in heaven:

Only one mistake, Ezra!
You should have talked
to women

Poetry must be at least
as powerful as music, but
I am not sure that
it is possible

10.
People visit, and I am
        shaken

(9)

° George Oppen ° 2811 Polk Street ° San Francisco, California 94109 °

'Clarity' means, among other things, to know how the words come to meaning.

~~-- . to experience~~

to experience how the words come to meaning

~~a note to Pound in heaven:~~

Only one mistake, Ezra! You should have talked to women

Poetry must be at least as graceful as music, but I am not sure that it is possible

11.
Our little bird: I
feel all my
boyhood in
him

12.
The world is black magic
The world is half magic

13.
Bach: The B minor mass!
I wept because it says
everything that can
ever be said

14.
Once the singing was
    and is[1]

15.

We are entering a new era and nothing will be the same in the storm (written while that storm was blowing

(post post modern)

16.
The universe moved
and we moved
in this monstrosity

17a.
Cortez arrives.
    he is absolutely lost

at an unknown shore.
    and he is enraptured[2]

(this is the nature of poetry

17b.
The poem:

Cortez arrives at an unknown shore
he is absolutely lost
and he is enraptured

17c.
Cortez arrives at an unknown shore
he is utterly lost
but he is enraptured

18.
Rezi's last poems:
just names, and the words
themselves
carry meaning   .   somehow

19a.
These ordinary words
    come to mean
    everything

In a way I live on words, forget words

19b.

The middle class boy to die in a foxhole like a dog

20.
Poetry is related to
music and cadence and therefore to the
force of events

21.
Hopkins   "my piece of being"[3]

22.
Poetry is the word that comes to music

23.

The tamed ~~stones~~
stones of the villages

24.
Music: out of these
houses to come forth

25.

tamed stones of ourselves

26.
The universe moved
and we move
In this monstrosity

Abbreviations

The following abbreviations are used for oft-cited sources:

ML Mary Oppen. *Meaning a Life: An Autobiography.* Santa Barbara, CA: Black Sparrow Press, 1978.

MP Burton Hatlen, ed. *George Oppen: Man and Poet.* Orono, ME: National Poetry Foundation, 1981.

NCP George Oppen. *New Collected Poems.* Ed. Michael Davidson. Preface by Eliot Weinberger. New York: New Directions, 2002.

SL George Oppen. *The Selected Letters of George Oppen.* Ed. Rachel Blau DuPlessis. Durham, NC: Duke University Press, 1990.

SP George Oppen. *Selected Poems.* Ed. Robert Creeley. New York: New Directions, 2003.

UCSD Archive for New Poetry, Mandeville Special Collections Library, University of California, San Diego

Notes

INTRODUCTION

1. Hugh Kenner, quoted from dust jacket of George Oppen, *Collected Poems* (New York: New Directions, 1975). I have updated citations in this volume to comply with more recent editions of Oppen's poetry (see abbreviations).

2. *The Best American Poetry 2002,* ed. Robert Creeley, series ed. David Lehman (New York. Scribner Poetry, 2002), 130–35.

3. *New Collected Poems,* ed. Michael Davidson (New York: New Directions, 2002); *Selected Poems,* ed. Robert Creeley (New York: New Directions, 2004).

4. From "A Narrative" (*NCP* 156; *SP* 78). Further citations are parenthetical.

5. From "The Mind's Own Place," p. 30 of the present volume.

6. Introducing her edition of Oppen's letters, Rachel Blau DuPlessis: "The combination of letters and . . . papers will, in *toto,* constitute Oppen's 'selected essays.' Oppen's complex, and constantly renegotiated rejection of public stances, his intricate and oblique dealings with fame, as well as his fascination with questioning and conversation, make consistent and characteristic his choice of these mediums for his essayistic writing" (*SL* x).

7. Important discussions of Objectivist poetry include Michael Heller's *Convictions' Net of Branches: Essays on the Objectivist Poets and Poetry* (Carbondale: Southern Illinois University Press, 1985), and a more recent collection edited by Rachel Blau DuPlessis and Peter Quartermain, *The Objectivist Nexus: Essays in Cultural Poetics* (Tuscaloosa: University of Alabama Press, 1999). Norman Finkelstein, in *Not One of Them in Place: Modern Poetry and Jewish American Identity* (Albany: State University of New York Press, 2001), and Stephen Fredman, in *A Menorah for Athena: Charles Reznikoff and the Dilemmas of Objectivist Poetry* (Chicago: University of Chicago Press, 2001), both provide admirable and long overdue accounts of Objectivist poetry's relationship to questions of Jewish and Jewish-American identity.

8. Oppen was the only one in the group to have some measure of financial flexibility. Zukofsky grew up as the son of immigrants speaking Yiddish on New York City's Lower East Side, where Reznikoff also lived; Rakosi was himself an immigrant. Niedecker was the rural exception; she lived on a modest farm in Wisconsin.

9. See, for example, DuPlessis: "One of the largest differences between Oppen and Pound is that Pound was perplexed by, and resistant to, historical fluidity and its demands on praxis. He wanted things settled once and for all. Oppen did not resist that fluidity, but was always fascinated with how the dimensions of 'want' changed and could be reassessed" ("Objectivist Poetics and Political Vision: A Study of Oppen and Pound," in *MP* 139). Peter Nicholls seeks a similar distinction in locating Oppen—and Objectivism in general—in a temporal and conceptual interstice between the totalizing platitudes of Modernism proper and the less autocratic, more open-ended inquiries typical of postmodernity: in "Modernizing Modernism: From Pound to Oppen," *Critical Quarterly* 44, no. 2 (Summer 2002): 41–58.

10. Louis Zukofsky, *Prepositions: The Collected Critical Essays of Louis Zukofsky,* expanded ed. (Berkeley and Los Angeles: University of California Press, 1981), 12.

11. It could be argued that the same was the case for Zukofsky, as his critical compliment to his poetry was unconventional at best: he described his magisterial study *Bottom: On Shakespeare* (Berkeley and Los Angeles: University of California Press, 1963)—by far the most voluminous and sustained piece of criticism by any Objectivist poet—as a long poem, and the collection of his essays published in 1967 is as stylistically complex as any of his poems. "A poet finds continuously present analysis of his work preferable to criticism so-called," Zukofsky wrote as a kind of defense of his obdurate prose style. "Yet what other criticism exclusive of his poem seems permissible?" (*Prepositions,* 14). In their collective critical reticence, the Objectivist group as a whole might be seen as having shared this sentiment.

12. Edward Hirsch, *Washington Post Book World,* November 23, 2003, T12.

13. See Oppen's letter to June Oppen Degnan (*SL* 57–58), in which he discusses the essay and Charles Humboldt's suggestions for revision. Also, see Oppen's uncharacteristically vitriolic response to Humboldt's critique (*SL* 59–61).

14. *The Letters of John Keats, 1814–1821,* ed. Hyder Edward Rollins (Cambridge, MA: Harvard University Press, 1958), 193.

15. *ML* no doubt remains the primary source for biographical information on Oppen. Other resources provide more linear and exhaustive accounts than mine here: Rachel Blau DuPlessis's introduction to *SL* (especially x–xx), as well as her brief introductions to each year of correspondence; Michael Davidson's introduction to *NCP* (xv–xxviii); Jeffrey Peterson, "George Oppen," in *Dictionary of Literary Biography: American Poets since World War II*, 4th series, ed. Joseph Conte et al. (Farmington Hills, MI: Gale Research, 1996), 188–206; Joseph G. Kronick's biographical note on the University of Chicago's Modern American Poetry Web site (www.english.uiuc.edu/maps/poets/m_r/oppen/life.html); and Rachel Blau DuPlessis's chronology of Oppen's life, in *SP* (192–98). Peter Nicholls gives an important and groundbreaking account of the Oppens' time in Mexico, in "George Oppen in Exile: Mexico and Maritain (for Linda Oppen)," *Journal of American Studies* 39, no. 1 (April

2005): 1–18. His critical biography of Oppen, is an equally groundbreaking work: *George Oppen and the Fate of Modernism* (New York: Oxford University Press, 2007).

16. Again, see Nicholls, "George Oppen in Exile," for an excellent survey of the Oppens' time in Mexico.

17. See John Taggart, "Walk Out: Rereading George Oppen," *Chicago Review* 44, no. 2 (1998): 29–93. Taggart takes some questionable interpretive liberties in his discussion of Oppen's Jewish identity—not the least of which involves his reading of Oppen's response to Jabès's work—yet it remains as compelling an essay as it is a controversial one.

18. George Oppen, "An Adequate Vision: A George Oppen Daybook," ed. Michael Davidson, *Ironwood* 26 (1985): 5–35. Davidson's selection, like all selections before mine, is culled primarily from the "Notes, Jottings, etc." series in the archive, and follows no authorial parameters of organization. It is thus not a "Daybook" per se, although I am using the term for Oppen's bound materials nonetheless.

19. Michael Davidson, "Palimtexts: Postmodern Poetry and the Material Text," in *Postmodern Genres,* ed. Marjorie Perloff (Norman: University of Oklahoma Press, 1989), 80.

THREE POETS

1. Ginsberg's poem is dedicated to his mother, Naomi Ginsberg (1894–1956), and recounts her struggles with mental illness.

2. Charles Olson, *The Maximus Poems,* ed. George Butterick (Berkeley and Los Angeles: University of California Press, 1983), 172.

3. Ibid., 176.

4. From "I, Mencius, Pupil of the Master . . ." in *The Distances,* 61.

5. From "The Praises," ibid., 25.

6. From "The Kingfishers," ibid., 8.

7. Rapallo, a small city in the Liguria region of Italy, was Pound's place of residence from 1924 to 1945. Regarding "the Valley of Mexico": in 1951, Olson spent six months on the Yucatan Peninsula researching Mayan culture and art. The experience exerted a lasting influence on Olson's thought and writing, as reflected in the lines Oppen quotes here.

8. From "As the Dead Prey upon Us," in *The Distances,* 78.

9. From *In Cold Hell, in Thicket,* ibid., 30.

10. Michael McClure, *Hymns to St. Geryon and Dark Brown* (San Francisco: Grey Fox, 1980), 86.

11. Ibid., 62: "I break/THRU THRU THRU THRU/the size of any/STAR!"

12. Donald Allen, ed., *The New American Poetry, 1945–1960* (New York: Grove Press, 1961), 336.

THE MIND'S OWN PLACE

1. John Singer Sargent (1856–1925), American portraitist and painter; Auguste Renoir (1841–1919), French impressionist painter.

2. Oppen is paraphrasing, not entirely faithfully, a recurrent image in Bertrand Russell's *The Problems of Philosophy* used to illustrate the epistemological complications of traditional philosophy. In chapter 1 ("Appearance and Reality"), for example:

> It seems to me that I am now sitting in a chair, at a table of a certain shape, on which I see sheets of paper with writing or print. By turning my head I see out of the window buildings and clouds and the sun. I believe that the sun is about ninety-three million miles from the earth; that it is a hot globe many times bigger than the earth; that, owing to the earth's rotation, it rises every morning, and will continue to do so for an indefinite time in the future. I believe that, if any other normal person comes into my room, he will see the same chairs and tables and books and papers as I see, and that the table which I see is the same as the table which I feel pressing against my arm. All this seems to be so evident as to be hardly worth stating, except in answer to a man who doubts whether I know anything. Yet all this may be reasonably doubted, and all of it requires much careful discussion before we can be sure that we have stated it in a form that is wholly true.

Bertrand Russell, *The Problems of Philosophy* (New York: Oxford University Press, 1959), 7–8. Again, in chapter 3 ("The Nature of Matter"):

> [I]t is rational to believe that our sense-data—for example, those which we regard as associated with my table—are really signs of the existence of something independent of us and our perceptions. That is to say, over and above the sensations of colour, hardness, noise, and so on, which make up the appearance of the table to me, I assume that there is something else, *of* which these things are appearances. The colour ceases to exist if I shut my eyes, the sensation of hardness ceases to exist if I remove my arm from contact with the table, the sound ceases to exist if I cease to rap the table with my knuckles. But I do not believe that when all these things cease the table ceases. On the contrary, I believe that it is because the table exists continuously that all these sense-data will reappear when I open my eyes, replace my arm, and begin again to rap with my knuckles." (27)

3. Oppen's adaptation of Heraclitus's fragment number 7, translated by G. S. Kirk thus: "If all existing things were to become smoke the nostrils would distinguish them." See G. S. Kirk, ed., *Heraclitus: The Cosmic Fragments* (New York: Cambridge University Press, 1959), 232. Oppen later used the fragment as the title to a poem in *Primitive* (*NCP* 274).

4. The *dolce stil novo,* or "sweet new style," was the mellifluous style of Dante's early philosophical love poetry, as well as that of other Italian poets in the late thirteenth century. The phrase itself comes from Dante's *Purgatorio* 24.57.

5. Vachel Lindsay (1879–1931); Carl Sandburg (1878–1967); Alfred Kreym-

borg (1883–1966); William Carlos Williams (1883–1963). The "Ash Can" school was founded (loosely) by painter Robert Henri (1865–1929) in 1891 in Philadelphia. The group's dictum was "art for life's sake" and their aesthetics centered largely on subject matter, rather than form and/or style (see Oppen's comment on Sandburg's poetry).

6. The phrase is misidentified as Williams's; it actually occurs in Charles Olson's essay "Projective Verse," where Olsen in turn attributes it to Robert Creeley. Charles Olson, *Collected Prose,* ed. Donald Allen and Benjamin Friedlander (Berkeley and Los Angeles: University of California Press, 1997), 240. Oppen may have read the phrase in Williams's *Autobiography,* however, and misattributed it thus.

7. See "West" (*NCP* 208; *SP* 124): "In wrath we await // The rare poetic / Of veracity that huge art whose geometric / Light seems not its own in that most dense world West and East / Have denied have hated have wandered in   *precariousness.*"

8. The poem is Levertov's "Matins," in *The Jacob's Ladder* (New York: New Directions, 1961), 57.

9. "Williams was a populist," Oppen says to Burton Hatlen and Tom Mandel in an interview, "but he really didn't know what he was talking about" (*MP* 25). The subject is political poetry, and Oppen is contrasting Williams's populism to Pound's elitism.

10. A commonly cited proverb in Chinese Buddhism. Oppen's source is unknown.

11. A term used by British journalists to refer to a diverse (and otherwise unorganized) group of politically radical British novelists and playwrights. The term gained prominence in the mainstream press after a press relase for the first performance of John Osborne's 1956 play *Look Back in Anger* used it to describe the play's author.

12. "DAR" refers to the Daughters of the American Revolution.

13. Oppen misappropriates (purposefully) the famous lines from John Donne's "Meditation 17" (1624): "No man is an island, entire of itself; every man is a piece of the Continent, a part of the main . . ."

14. From Brecht's poem "To Those Born Later" ("An Die Nachgeborenen"): "What kind of times are they, when / A talk about trees is almost a crime / Because it implies silence about so many horrors?" See *Bertolt Brecht Poems, 1913–1956,* ed. John Willett and Ralph Manheim (New York: Methuen, 1976), 318.

15. Also in the Hatlen/Mandel interview, in response to a question regarding his return to the writing of poetry, Oppen says: "Rome had recently burned, so there was no reason not to fiddle" (*MP* 34).

16. "We want bread and roses" is a slogan associated with a textile strike that took place in Lawrence, Massachusetts, in 1912. "Let a thousand flowers bloom" is a misquotation of Mao's 1957 slogan "Let a hundred flowers bloom; let a hundred schools of thought contend."

17. In William Stafford, *Stories That Could Be True: New and Collected Po-*

ems (New York: Harper and Row, 1977), 107. Incidentally, the line appears in the poem as a quotation of the speaker's father's advice.

18. Robert Duncan (1919–88). The quotation is from an unknown source.

19. Ironic miscontrual of American civil war general William Tecumseh Sherman's response to the notion that he might be drawn into the 1884 presidential race: "If drafted, I will not run; if nominated, I will not accept; if elected, I will not serve."

ON ARMAND SCHWERNER

1. The final lines of "prologue in six parts" (section 6), reprinted in Armand Schwerner, *Selected Shorter Poems* (San Diego: Junction Press, 1999), 74.

2. The final lines of section 3 of ibid., 69.

3. The final lines of section 2 of "the violence around us," in ibid., 41.

A NOTE ON TOM MCGRATH ETC.

1. Sidney Finkelstein (1909–74) was an art, music, and cultural critic affiliated, like McGrath, with the Communist Party in the United States, and like McGrath called to testify before HUAC in 1974. With the name Joe Hecht, Oppen is most likely referring to Ben Hecht (1894–1964), screenwriter, novelist, Zionist, and human rights activist. It is possible (but unlikely) that Joe Hecht is the Polish-Parisian painter and printmaker Joseph Hecht (1891–1951), who is considered by some, despite official records, to have died in a Nazi death camp during World War II. Oppen may have met him while living in France in the early 1930s, but there are no records of any such meeting. Charles Humboldt (1910–64) was editor, with McGrath, of *Masses and Mainstream.*

A LETTER

1. The poem opens:

"out of poverty
to begin

again"   impoverished

of tone of pose that common
wealth

of parlance   Who
so poor the words . . . (*NCP* 220; *SP* 121)

The opening citation is from Charles Simic's poem "White" (in *White* [Moorhead, MN: New River Press, 1972], 11). "White" is a long poem and these are its opening lines.

2. Oppen, in a letter to Robert Duncan: "The one connection between us in our work is that—the one essential tie—is this: that we do not know before we complete the poem. Neither of us write[s] what we already know, and of course that's the essential life of the poem" (*SL* 270).

NON-RESISTANCE, ETC. OR: OF THE GUILTLESS

1. On April 22, 1945, Oppen was seriously injured in a foxhole while serving in Alsace. He was the only one of the three men in the foxhole to have survived the direct attack.

STATEMENT ON POETICS

1. The poem was later revised, and comprises the last ten lines of "To Make Much," in *Primitive* (*NCP* 271–72). The stanza now reads:

> to the shining
> of rails in the night
> the shining way the way away
> from home arrow in the air
> hat-brim fluttered in the air as she ran
> forward and it seemed so beautiful
> the sun-lit air was no dream all's wild
> out there as we unlikely
> image of love found the way
> away from home

Given Oppen's comments following his reading, the revisions seem telling.

2. In "The Mind's Own Place," p. 32 in the present volume.

3. See "Song, the Winds of Downhill": "sliding // hands and heels beyond the residential / lots   the plots   it is a poem // which may be sung / may well be sung" (*NCP* 220; *SP* 129).

DAYBOOK I

Source: UCSD 16, 19, 1.

1. *Salt of the Earth* (1954) was a film by blacklisted director Herbert J. Biberman (1900–1971) that featured a blacklisted cast and crew. The only American

film to be blacklisted, *Salt of the Earth* tells the story of a 1950 zinc miners strike in New Mexico.

2. Cf. "A Language of New York" (*NCP* 116; *SP* 51).

3. On various occasions, Oppen speaks of Auden in similarly critical terms, although it bears noting that Oppen regarded as one of the greatest limitations of twentieth-century poetry its superficial, stylistic postures. See, for example, *NCP* 101; *SP* 37.

4. Louis Zukofsky (1904–78), poet and longtime friend of Oppen's.

5. Cf. "Guest Room" (*NCP* 107; *SP* 42). Oppen's reference, as he explains in a 1963 letter to June Oppen Degnan, is to "Seville and George of San Mateo . . . the dinner parties of San Mateo" and the wealth of his childhood (see *SL* 94 as well as Davidson's note on the poem, *NCP* 374).

6. "*Truth follows / The existence of something*" is Oppen's translation of Aquinas's "veritas sequitor esse rerum." Oppen uses the phrase as an epigraph to "Psalm" (*NCP* 99; *SP* 36).

7. Eliphas Lévi was the pseudonym of Alphonse Louis Constant (1810–75). An occultist and a writer on Masonic Freemasonry, he was known for books on "transcendental magic."

8. Oppen's reference is to Balzac's short stories "Seraphita" and "Louis Lambert."

9. "Leviathan" is a poem of Oppen's (*NCP* 59; *SP* 30); Simone Weil (1909–43) was a French philosopher, political activist, and mystic. The first poem in Oppen's *Seascape: Needle's Eye* is entitled "From a Phrase of Simone Weil's and Some Words of Hegel's" (*NCP* 21; *SP* 121), and Oppen may be referring here to an earlier draft of that poem.

10. The term *bric-a-brac* occurs in much of Henry Miller's writing, although it is unclear to which of Miller's works Oppen is referring.

11. Oppen repeats the meditation on "bric-a-brac" at the bottom of a page containing a draft of "Eros" (*NCP* 120–21), located nearby this sheet:

> What are these people like
> And what else matters?
> in their hands and country
> and his arms
> The opening and closing
> Of doors, the keys and the locks,
> The machines, the buildings of walls
> And the destruction of walls.
>
> deluge of bric-a-brac is reality &
> then what else matters?

The page concludes (the words circled): "The deluge / of bric-a-brac / in his hands // a bric-a-brac reality" (see my selection in *Germ* 3 [Spring 1999]: 209, where this latter page is reproduced). Oppen's sense of bric-a-brac—possibly a reflection on the very practice of writing that produced such heteroglossic pages as these—provides the justification for reproducing it here as is, as does the curious inclusion of a number series (not a "discrete" series, but a continuous one, as it were). The references to Henry Miller, Balzac, Simone Weil, and Leviathan likely comprise a reading list, rather than references to specific poems (i.e., "Leviathan" [*NCP* 89; *SP* 30] and "From a Phrase of Simone Weil's and Some Words of Hegel's" [*NCP* 211; *SP* 121]).

12. "Beauty is truth, truth beauty—that is all / Ye know on earth, and all ye need to know" are the penultimate and ultimate lines of Keats's "Ode on a Grecian Urn."

13. C. P. Snow (1905–80) introduced Charles Reznikoff's *By the Waters of Manhattan* (New York: New Directions, 1962); May Swenson's (1913–89) praise of Reznikoff's work appeared on the same volume's back cover.

14. Oppen is likely referring to the early writing of 1990 Nobel laureate Octavio Paz (1914–98), preeminent Mexican poet, essayist, and diplomat. Often under the influence of surrealism, Paz's early work dealt in elaborate symbolic and at times hallucinatory images.

15. Cf. "A Language of New York" (*NCP* 114–19; *SP* 49–54), where Oppen both extends and qualifies his thoughts about the "ugliness" of New York City. The poem formed the basis of "Of Being Numerous" (*NCP* 163–88; *SP* 83–110).

16. Oppen's reference is Jean Genet (1910–86), specifically his play *Le Balcon* (1956), upon which he comments at length in Daybook III.

17. A reference to Oscar Lewis, *The Children of Sanchez: Autobiography of a Mexican Family* (New York: Random House, 1961).

18. "The English in Virginia" is the subtitle of section 74 ("The English in Virginia, April 1607") of Charles Reznikoff's "Jerusalem the Golden," a section based on Reznikoff's reading of the writings of Captain John Smith, bearing an authorial footnote to that effect. See Reznikoff, *Poems, 1918–1975: The Complete Poems of Charles Reznikoff,* ed. Seamus Cooney (Santa Barbara, CA: Black Sparrow Press, 1989), 122.

19. Possibly Michael Ponce de Leon (1922–), American painter and visual artist.

20. Cf. "The Occurrences" (*NCP* 144).

21. See *SL* 85, Oppen writing to June Oppen Degnan: "Not to deny that many people will assert that they feel confronted by Bronk. But since Bronk's attitudes take off from Gödel, Heisenberg, Einstein, and theirs from Newtonian mechanics (d. 1727), their belief that they are in some way ahead of him is probably an illusion. In any case, how long can it last—speaking of the 'two cultures'?" The reference is to a book by C. P. Snow, whose introduction to Charles Reznikoff's *By the Waters of Manhattan* Oppen was at first opposed to (and of which he was at first critical), although he was later more sympathetic (see note on Snow and Swenson above). See C. P. Snow, *The Two Cultures* (Cambridge: Cambridge University Press, 1993). First published in 1959, Snow's is a now

well-known account (and critique) of the division between the sciences and the humanities.

22. "a bout" is most likely a typographical error, although I've preserved it here for the sake of the curious pun, which Oppen may or may not have intended.

23. *"The truth shall make us free"*: echoes John 8:31, 32: "If you continue in my word, then you are my disciples indeed, and you shall know the truth, and the truth shall make you free." The phrase that Oppen quotes was also used as an ironic slogan by German revisionist historians who wished to deny the Holocaust, as its German formulation—"Warheit macht Frei"—echoes the Nazi Party dictum "Arbeit macht Frei" ("Work will set you free"). Given the context here, however, it is unlikely that Oppen is referring to the latter usage.

DAYBOOK II:I

Source: UCSD 16, 19, 2.

1. See Oppen's 1962 letter to Max and Anita Pepper (*SL* 62–66). Although arguments about art's relationship to politics preoccupied Oppen throughout his life and career, they were particularly of issue in the early 1960s, when much of the material in this Daybook was likely composed.

2. Oppen is referring to "Not My Loneliness, but Ours," from William Bronk's *The World, the Worldless* (New York: New Directions, 1964), 17.

3. Cf. "Night Scene" (*NCP* 137).

4. Oppen's half-sister, June Oppen Degnan, political activist and publisher of the *San Francisco Review.*

5. Oppen's comments here are offset by numerous others elsewhere, although it still would be a mistake to ignore Oppen's sometimes less than enlightened comments on gender. Peter Quartermain offers an account of Oppen's encouragement and support of women writers (uncharacteristic for male poets at the time) in "Excerpts from 'Conversations with One's Peers': George Oppen and some Women Writers," taken from his 1996 George Oppen Memorial Lecture, presented at the First Unitarian Church, San Francisco, December 5, 1996. In the *Poetry Center and American Poetry Archive News* 13 (San Francisco: Poetry Center and American Poetry Archives, 1997), 11–14. See also below, where Oppen comments more generally on women's history.

6. Michael Davidson provides an engaging reading of this page, and the section from Oppen's poem "Route" (*NCP* 194) that evolves from it, in "Palimtexts: Postmodern Poetry and the Material Text," *Genre* 20, nos. 3–4 (1987): 307–27.

7. Cf. section 10 of "Of Being Numerous" (*NCP* 167; *SP* 88).

8. Harvey Shapiro (1924–), poet and longtime editor of the *New York Times Book Review.*

9. For "limits of life," see these lines from "Guest Room" (*NCP* 109; *SP* 44):

It is the courage of the rich

Who are an *avant garde*

Near the limits of life—Like theirs

My abilities
Are ridiculous:

To go perhaps unarmed
And unarmored, to return

Now to the old questions—

10. The first major translation into English of René Char's poetry appeared in 1956 (with translations by William Carlos Williams, W. S. Merwin, and James Wright, among others). Still, Oppen seems more to be offering a general commentary on Char and/or modern French poetry than discussing a particular translation. See *Hypnos Waking: Poetry and Prose of René Char,* ed. and trans. Jackson Matthews et al. (New York: Random House, 1956).

11. For "the funny little core of myself," see *NCP* 93.

12. In a letter to Diane Wakoski (1965), Oppen touches on some of the issues raised here: "Mary said to some rather painful visitors who gingerly examined this example of what they had almost feared might be going on—Mary said; there are beginnings, something might happen, whereas the *New Yorker* and *Esquire* are a dead end, and a crushing weight. [hard paragraph break] With which I agree. [hard paragraph break] It seems to me these dreams are more becoming to the Young Ladies than to the men" (*SL* 110).

13. John Howard Lawson (1894–1977), playwright, screenwriter, founder, with Lester Cole and Samuel Ortiz, of the Screen Writers' Guild, and prominent member of the blacklisted Hollywood Ten. Miller is Henry Miller.

14. Oppen misquotes the last line from Bronk's "Boolean Algebra: $X^2 = X$": "it is as though / an amoeba should read to us, or snakes should sing." *The World, the Worldless,* 36. Oppen meditates more on this poem below.

15. Poets Cid Corman (1924–2004) and Louis Zukofsky (1904–78).

16. The initials in this sentence refer to John Howard Lawson.

17. Incidentally, Oppen was invited to lunch by one-time presidential hopeful Eugene McCarthy in 1970. Writing to Robert Creeley: "[M]y sister a short while ago asking me to have lunch with Gene McCarthy, assuring me for the nth time that he wanted above all else in this world to converse with poets—I said, well, make it Duncan, Creeley, Oppen" (*SL* 213). Although Oppen's sister, June Oppen Degnan, served as the national finance chairman for McCarthy's campaign for the Democratic nomination in 1968, the lunch never took place.

18. Oppen often returned to pages—sometimes years later—to amend and/or revise his thoughts, or to gather phrases, stanzas, fragments and the like for po-

ems. This is among the few places, however, where he so explicitly marks the return. This transcription combines two of Oppen's pages, one of which appears in holograph at the beginning of this section. The second draft is the one I used to transcribe the prose of the first two paragraphs. I felt it nonetheless important to preserve Oppen's "addition" and dating at the bottom of the page.

19. Cf. "World-Word" (*NCP* 159).

DAYBOOK II:II

Source: UCSD 16, 19, 3.

1. Oppen's citation of Eckhart is correct: the phrase appears near the end of "Being Is More Than Life," a sermon on mortality and immortality, the latter identified with a knowledge of God. See *Meister Eckhart: A Modern Translation,* trans. Raymond Bernard Blakney (New York: Harper and Brothers, 1957), 172.

2. And, indeed, Oppen could afford it: his inheritance upon his twenty-first birthday of a substantial sum of money allowed him and Mary to travel widely, and facilitated their move to Mexico and their subsequent return. See *ML,* where Mary Oppen frequently addresses this inheritance and its allowances (so to speak).

3. The page is ripped at the top and in the middle. I have conjectured about missing text where appropriate.

DAYBOOK II:III

Source: UCSD 16, 19, 4.

1. Oppen refers to M. D. Herder Norton, translator of Rilke and others. Oppen owned a copy of Norton's translation of *Sonnets to Orpheus* (New York: W. W. Norton, 1942), although the line Oppen quotes does not appear there.

2. The above quotation is likely from Maritain's *Creative Intuition in Art and Poetry* (Princeton, NJ: Princeton University Press, 1981). The book was central to Oppen's thought in the mid- to late 1960s.

3. *NCP* 114; *SP* 49; and *NCP* 164; *SP* 84.

4. Cf. "That Land," from "Five Poems about Poetry" (*NCP* 103; *SP* 39).

5. The words in quotes are a summary of one line of thinking in Aleksandr Esenin-Volpin, *A Leaf of Spring,* trans. George Reavey (New York: Praeger, 1961). Oppen refers to Esenin-Volpin (1924–) throughout the Daybooks.

6. The direct reference is to Moore's poem "The Jerboa." See *The Complete Poems of Marianne Moore* (New York: Macmillan/Viking Press, 1967), 10.

7. The last sentence in Ludwig Wittgenstein, *Tractatus Logico-Philosophicus:* "Wovon man nicht sprechen kann, darüber muß man schweigen."

8. Cf. Andrew Marvell, "To His Coy Mistress," ll. 1–2: "Had we but world enough, and time, / This coyness, Lady, were no crime."

9. "The Zulu Girl" is the title of a poem by Oppen (*NCP* 148).

10. Marisol Escobar (1930–), sculptor and artist associated with the pop art movement in New York City in the 1960s.

11. Oppen is possibly referring to one of a number of Marisol's works that originally appeared in her two Stable Gallery shows in the early 1960s, including her mixed media works *The Kennedys* (1960) and *The Family* (1963), the latter of which is a biting satire of the American middle class. See Nancy Grove's catalog for the 1991 Smithsonian exhibition, *Magical Mixtures: Marisol Portrait Sculpture* (Washington, DC: Smithsonian Institution Press, 1991).

12. The poem is "prologue in six parts," in which Schwerner quotes lines from Oppen's "A Narrative," and draws a parallel between Oppen and Akiba (from the Haggadah). Oppen comments on and critiques the poem in an August 1964 letter to Schwerner (*SL* 101–2), and quotes from it in a review of Schwerner's book in *Stony Brook* 3–4 (1969): 72, published in the present volume as "On Armand Schwerner."

13. Oppen is referring to William Carlos Williams's biography of his mother, *Yes, Mrs. Williams: A Personal Record of My Mother* (New York: McDoweel, Obolensky, 1959).

14. Oppen is parodying here the closing line of the first sonnet in Philip Sidney's *Astrophil and Stella:* "Fool said my Muse to me, look in thy heart and write."

15. The letter to which Oppen refers is not extant. Still, it is clear that by "Depression" Oppen means the historical event, and not psychological impairment.

16. Misspelling of Pamela Hansford Johnson (1912–81), English critic and writer of psychological novels. Johnson reviewed Wallace Fowlie, *A Reading of Proust* (Garden City, NY: Anchor Books, 1964).

17. Oppen refers to Schwerner's poem "Muck the Fuck":

> One room of the gray rat
> two room for the cowlick
> seven room for moose
> and Muck the Fuck to celebrate;
>
> he says: I fuck the moose
> with cowlick; the Grey rat
> bears the urine
> from room to room for the proper dance,
> slippery floor for the moose-mad;
>
> cheese in the graveyard
> where's it from?
> if you eat a plum
> milkem
>
> who's to be milked?
> moose to be mucked

by the gay-step Fuck
in the lacy web.
Bees in the mouth.

Room for the real.
Kitchen of shadows, bing.
If you don't sing
what's out there?

Rat moose cowlick prick
open your mouth a little bit
drapes are falling everywhere
Foot in your ears.

From *Selected Shorter Poems* (San Diego: Junction Press, 1999), 34.

18. "Boy's Room" is the title of a poem by Oppen (*NCP* 122; *SP* 55).

19. Cf. "That Land," from "Five Poems about Poetry" (*NCP* 103; *SP* 39).

DAYBOOK II:IV

Source: UCSD 16, 19, 5.

1. The specific book to which Oppen refers is most likely *This in Which,* while "Of Being Numerous," already partly underway when *This in Which* was published, would be the book (or long poem) of "just understanding it."

2. Likely from Jacques Maritain.

3. In lectures and articles, Maritain often identified communism as the ultimate manifestation of "anthropocentric rationalism," and often in sharply critical terms. In "A Faith to Live By," for instance: "Communism, which is the ultimate vicissitude of anthropocentric rationalism, endeavors indeed to save faith in man and offers itself as the last chance of optimism. Its optimism, however, is the optimism of matter's and technique's titanic and coercive energies, its man is totally absorbed in the life of a truthless and loveless god who is human dehumanised community. Faith in man, but in what kind of man? The real man, the human person, is devoured by an idol of man." "A Faith to Live By," in the Jacques Maritain Papers, Jacques Maritain Center Web site, University of Notre Dame, www.nd.edu/Departments/Maritain/jm0106 (accessed March 12, 2007).

4. Ethel Schwabacher (1903–84), painter, and Oppen's cousin.

5. Leni Kaplan, wife of George Kaplan. The two were friends of the Oppens in the 1960s.

6. Oppen is commenting on his poem "A Narrative" (*NCP* 150–56; *SP* 72–78), especially the closing stanzas (*NCP* 156; *SP* 78).

7. The quote from Baldwin is one of his most often cited. It first appeared in the *New York Times,* June 1, 1964.

8. "Billy" is William Bronk (1918–99).

9. The source of this phrase is unknown.

10. This passage was most likely written before 1965, as by then Oppen, following precedents established by the militant black press, had abandoned using the term "Negro."

11. Oppen could be speaking of Louis Zukofsky here, whom he had accused of cleverness on more than one occasion. It is also possible that the passage refers to Robert Creeley, especially given the parodic enjambment.

12. LeRoi Jones, later Amiri Baraka (1934–), poet, playwright critic, and activist.

13. Again, Oppen's comments are dated by his description of the SNCC (Student Nonviolent Coordinating Committee, 1960–70, civil rights group founded by black students in 1960 at Shaw University in Raleigh, NC), whose philosophy became much more militant after 1966, when Stokely Charmichael replaced John Lewis as chairman, fracturing the movement.

14. Oppen quotes the phrase "Veritas sequitur esse rerum" ("Truth follows from the existence of things") as an epigraph to "Psalm" (*NCP* 99; *SP* 36), and quotes it throughout both Daybooks and Papers.

15. Oppen refers to and/or cites Blake's poem "Tyger" (from *Songs of Experience*) often in his writings, poetic and otherwise. See, especially, "The Poem" (*NCP* 270; *SP* 164).

16. Cf. the first section of "A Language of New York" (*NCP* 114; *SP* 49), and the second section of "Of Being Numerous" (*NCP* 164; *SP* 84).

17. *This in Which* bears two flyleaf quotations, one from Heidegger ("the arduous path of appearance") and the other from Robert A. Heinlein, *The Unpleasant Profession of Jonathan Hoag* (New York: Grove Press, 1959):

> "Wait a minute," Randall said insistently. "Are you trying to describe the creation of the world—the universe?"
> "What else?"
> "But—damn it, this is preposterous! I asked for an explanation of the things that have just happened to *us*."
> "I told you that you would not like the explanation." (quoted in *NCP* 92)

It is unclear to whom Oppen is writing here.

18. Again, Leni Kaplan.

19. At roughly the age of twenty, George and Mary hitchhiked across the United States, ending up in New York, where they met Reznikoff, Zukofsky, and others. Still, it is clearly to their experiences outside of East Coast literary circles to which Oppen here refers.

20. Gottfried Wilhelm Leibniz (1646–1716), rationalist philosopher, mentions on numerous occasions the "undeniability of the body" and/or "material world" as a complication of earlier idealist philosophies.

21. See also, again, *NCP* 114 and 164; *SP* 49 and 84.

22. It is unclear to whom Oppen is referring.

23. A reference to Marianne Moore's poem "Poetry": I, too, dislike it / Reading it, however, with a perfect contempt for it, one discovers in / it, after all, a place for the genuine." *The Complete Poems of Marianne Moore* (New York: Macmillan / Viking Press, 1967), 36.

24. Oppen attributes this quotation to Maritain—"We awake in the same moment to ourselves and to things"—and uses it as an epigraph to *The Materials* (*NCP* 38). The phrase does not appear verbatim in Maritain's *Creative Intuition in Art and Poetry* (Cleveland: Meridian Press, 1954), but appears to be a summary of Maritain's reflections on "Things and the Creative Self," the third of four sections that comprise the book's first chapter, "Poetry, Man, and Things." Oppen often misremembered and/or misattributed quotations and phrases from the work of others. See *SL* 134–37, where Oppen reflects upon this tendency apropos his reading of the first essay in Heidegger's *Essays on Metaphysics: Identity and Difference.*

25. June Oppen Degnan, Oppen's half-sister and life-long confidant. Degnan was active in literary, artistic, and political circles throughout her life, publishing the *San Francisco Review* (which, with New Directions, published Oppen's second and third books), and later serving as national finance chairperson for Eugene McCarthy's presidential campaign (1967–69), as vice-chairperson of George McGovern's presidential campaign (1970–72), and as a member of the Democratic National Committee (1972–80).

DAYBOOK II:V

Source: UCSD 16, 19, 6.

1. Oppen claimed in a letter to his daughter, Linda, and her then husband, Alex Maurelatos, that he "thought [the Warren Report] altogether conclusive" in its finding regarding the assassination of Kennedy, going on to note a curious parallel between James Joyce's *Ulysses* and the Warren document. This latter comparison emerges as well in "Armies of the Plain," wherein Oppen quotes from Jack Ruby's Warren Commission testimony. See *SL* 106–8; *NCP* 95–96.

2. Oppen misquotes the opening lines of Zukofsky's rendering of Catullus number 16: "Piping, beans, I'll go *whoosh* and I'll rumble you / pathic Aurelius and catamount Furius, / who mis my versicles with your poor tastes—" Louis Zukofsky, *Complete Short Poetry* (Baltimore: Johns Hopkins University Press, 1991), 253.

3. Oppen's handwriting is altogether illegible here.

4. Charles Tomlinson (1927–), British poet and a longtime correspondent of Oppen's. Tomlinson was strongly influenced in his poetics by Williams and the Objectivists.

5. See the opening lines of "Eros" (*NCP* 120–21).

6. Cf. "Eros."

7. Ibid.

8. Clearly this page served as a draft of the poem "Eros," but the additional commentary (contextual to the poem and otherwise) justifies its inclusion here nonetheless. Oppen's reference to Père-Lachaise is to a plaque at Père-Lachaise Cemetery in Paris commemorating the execution of 147 members of the Paris Commune there in 1871. See Davidson's notes for the poem (*NCP* 375).

9. Again, "Eros" (*NCP* 120).

10. Possibly a reference to Bernard Evslin (1922–93), screenwriter and producer of documentary films (most notably, *Cassius Clay* [1970]), and celebrated author of children's books, including *The Adventures of Ulysses* (New York: Scholastic Book Services, 1969). Then again, Oppen might be referring to preeminent James Joyce scholar Bernard Benstock, whose edited collection of scholarly articles on Joyce's novel, *Approaches to* Ulysses: *Ten Essays,* appeared in 1970 (Pittsburgh: University of Pittsburgh Press).

11. Edna St. Vincent Millay (1892–1950), American lyrical poet and first woman to receive the Pulitzer Prize for poetry (1923); Arthur Stuart-Menteth (A. S. M.) Hutchinson (1880–1971), British writer of best-selling romance novels.

12. Oppen's references to and citations of Plotinus here and throughout the Daybooks seem like reading notes.

13. *Macbeth* 3.11.13.

14. Oppen's citations of Esdras are correct: 2 Esdras 3:10–11.

15. Refrain of a ballade by François Villon, which can be translated as "Where are the snows of yesteryear?"

16. Cf. the opening lines of William Wordsworth's "The Rainbow:" "My heart leaps up when I behold / A rainbow in the sky . . ." *The Poetical Works of Wordsworth,* ed. Paul D. Sheats (Boston: Houghton Mifflin, 1982), 277.

17. Parody of the opening of William Blake's "Auguries of Innocence": "To see a World in a Grain of Sand / And a Heaven in a Wild Flower / Hold Infinity in the palm of your Hand / And Eternity in an hour." *The Complete Poetry and Prose of William Blake,* ed. David V. Erdman (Berkeley and Los Angeles: University of California Press, 1982), 490.

18. Cf. section 21 of "Of Being Numerous" (*NCP* 175; *SP* 96).

19. Cf. the second stanza of "The Occurrences" (*NCP* 144).

20. *Piers Plowman,* B version, passus 1, line 158; C version, passus 1, line 153. See William Langland, *Piers Plowman: A Parallel-Text Edition of the A, B, C, and Z Versions,* ed. A. V. C. Schmidt (London: Longman, 1995), vol. 1.

21. The reference is most likely to Allen Ginsberg.

22. The reference is to the fourth stanza of the poem "Dirge for Two Veterans": "I hear the great drums pounding, / And the small drums steady whirring, / And

every blow of the great convulsive drums, / strikes me through and through." Walt Whitman, *Complete Poetry and Collected Prose* (New York: Library of America, 1982), 448.

23. Plotinus's *Third Ennead,* seventh tractate, is entitled "Time and Eternity." The second section to which Oppen refers is a philosophical consideration of Eternity.

24. Illegible passage on the *New Yorker* magazine. Included are the words "unable to begin at the beginning," from "A Language of New York" and "Of Being Numerous" (*NCP* 114 and 170; *SP* 49 and 92): "Unable to begin / At the beginning, the fortunate / Find everything already here."

25. Cf. section 4 of "A Language of New York" (*NCP* 116; *SP* 51).

26. X. J. Kennedy, *An Introduction to Poetry,* the first edition of which appeared in 1966 (Boston: Little, Brown).

27. *The Cry for Freedom*—an anthology of speeches and writings from voices as diverse as Lyndon B. Johnson, Robert and John F. Kennedy, Malcolm X, and James Baldwin—appeared in 1969, and Oppen may be referring to this. See Frank J. Hale, ed., *The Cry for Freedom: An Anthology of the Best That Has Been Said and Written on Civil Rights since 1954* (New York: A. S. Barnes, 1969). His comments, however, suggest more a response to the general issue of civil rights than to a specific collection of writings.

28. The Heidegger quotes here and below are from *What Is Philosophy?* trans. William Kluback and Jean T. Wilde (Twayne Publishers, 1958). Oppen's page citations are correct.

29. "E" and "David" are poet-editor-translator Clayton Eshleman (1935–) and poet-critic David Antin (1932–). Antin's first book, *Definitions,* was published by Eshleman's Caterpillar Press in 1967, and reviewed by Oppen (see "A Review of David Antin's *Definitions*" in the present volume).

30. Cf. section 2 of "A Language of New York" (*NCP* 114; *SP* 49); and section 13 of "Of Being Numerous" (*NCP* 170; *SP* 91).

DAYBOOK III

Source: UCSD 16, 19, 7.

1. Oppen quotes the last line of Plotinus *Sixth* (and final) *Ennead*.

2. See Bronk's "Boolean Algebra: $X^2 = X$":

> Quantity is what is not. The truth
> is ignorant of numbers. The universe
> is one, is all; besides there is nothing. The square
> of one, the square of nothing, is only one,
> —or nothing. $X^2 = X$. The truth
> admits these values. What is other is not
> the truth

Zero and one. An algebra
of these alone expresses everything.

3. The addressee is unknown.

4. Debbie Reynolds (1932–) is a singer, actress, and Hollywood celebrity who appeared in over forty films between 1948 and 2005.

5. Aleksandr Esenin-Volpin, whose *Leaf of Spring* appeared in 1961 and included "A Free Philosophical Treatise," from which these lines are taken. See Aleksandr Esenin-Volpin, *A Leaf of Spring,* trans. George Reavey (New York: Praeger, 1961).

6. Cf. the opening lines of "From Virgil," section 5 of "Five Poems about Poetry" (*NCP* 104; *SP* 40).

7. Theodor Enslin (1925–), poet and longtime correspondent of Oppen's.

8. The page is quite clearly a draft of section 4 (subtitled "Parousia") from "Five Poems about Poetry," but I have included it nonetheless as it (also clearly) represents an attempt on Oppen's part to think certain aspects of the poem simultaneously. Given his tendency to cut and paste lines from one place to another, it is possible that Oppen used this leaf as a wellspring of sorts for numerous lines in the poem (as if the poem itself represented a filling in of the blanks between these here fairly discontinuous statements), as do the few pages that follow.

9. The reference is to the rhymed historical chronicles of Sweden composed (or at least committed to paper) in the late fifteenth century.

10. It is not clear to whom Oppen refers here.

11. *Bare* is likely a typographical error ("bear"). However, as this is a rare instance in which the mistake (if, indeed, it is a mistake) generates meanings which are germane to Oppen's thinking, I have left it as is.

12. From an unknown source.

13. A 1956 play by Jean Genet (see *SL* 161). *Le Balcon* (1956), influenced by Antonin Artaud's Theater of Cruelty, is set in an hallucinatory brothel wherein men indulge to excess fantastic and illusory roles (judges viciously punishing thieves, bureaucrats being seduced by Arab maidens) that become confused with the purportedly "real" roles of powerful men participating in a revolution taking place outside the brothel (Oppen's comments on the roles of Jacqueline Kennedy and others below presumably derive in part from his reading of the play). In a 1967 letter to Fredric Will (*SL* 161), Oppen mentions the play in the context of a discussion of freedom and social (economic) status, mentioning also "the Beats, the Hippies, or even being young" as forms of spectacular indulgence that, like the indulgent exhibited in Genet's play, simulate a kind of perverse social freedom.

14. Robert Duncan and Oppen—despite their mutual admiration and respect—often quarreled on issues fundamental to each one's respective poetics.

15. The precise reference is unclear, although the phrase may be derived from Cotton Mather's (in)famous *Wonders of the Invisible World.*

16. There is no poem in Oppen's oeuvre that could rightly be said to be com-

posed entirely in iambics, although according to the acknowledgments in the first edition of Oppen's *Collected Poems* (New York: New Directions, 1975), the *New Yorker* did publish "Bahamas" (*NCP* 131; *SP* 61). See *SL* 85–86, where Oppen discusses with June Oppen Degnan the possibility of submitting "Bahamas" and other poems both to the *New Yorker* and *Atlantic Monthly*.

17. Steven Schneider (1934–), nephew of Julia Zimet, both of whom were friends of the Oppens in Mexico. Schneider was a writer and translator of poetry and fiction, and sometimes used the pseudonym "Samuel Klominos."

18. Act 2, scene 4, of Moliere's *Le Bourgeoise Gentilhomme,* or *The Bourgeoise Gentleman,* consists of a comedic dialogue between two characters (including the eponymous one) about the nature of and differences between prose and verse.

19. Cf. section 21 of "Of Being Numerous" (*NCP* 175; *SP* 96).

20. Spoken by Ivan Karamazov in Fyodor Dostoyevsky's *The Brothers Karamazov:* "If God does not exist, then everything is permitted." Bergman is Ingmar Bergman.

21. Oppen is referring to Jean-Jacques Rousseau's *Discourse on the Origin of Inquality* (1754), wherein Rousseau sets out to refute the notion of the "natural man," set forth by Thomas Hobbes in *Leviathan* (1651).

22. Robinson Crusoe is a major figure in Oppen's work, especially in "Of Being Numerous" with the phrase "the shipwreck of the singular" (a phrase that Oppen repeats on numerous occasions in his prose and poetry alike). See, especially, section 6 (*NCP* 165–66; *SP* 86).

23. Steven Schneider.

24. The reference is to Genet's play (see note 13).

25. The source is unknown.

26. From the parable "Before the Law," told by the priest to the protagonist "K" in Franz Kafka's *The Trial:* a man waits outside an open door until the moment of his death, begging a guard to let him in. Before dying, he asks the guard why no one else ever came to the door. The guard's answer is quoted here.

27. From Marcel Proust's *Swann's Way.*

28. Likely from Heidegger's *Introduction to Metaphysics.* Heidegger dedicates about one-third of the first chapter of the book ("The Fundamental Question of Metaphysics") to the definition of the word *physis* and the identification of Being and *physis.* Martin Heidegger, *Introduction to Metaphysics,* trans. Gregory Fried and Richard Polt (New Haven, CT: Yale University Press, 2000), 14–19.

29. Source unknown.

30. Thomas Merton (1925–68), poet, writer, Trappist monk, and correspondent of Oppen's.

31. From Kafka's short story "The Tower of Babel."

32. A phrase of Chairman Mao Tse-tung's, uttered frequently during the Chinese Cultural Revolution.

33. "Andy" is Diane Meyer, Oppen's niece.

34. Cf. "World, World" (*NCP* 159).

DAYBOOK IV:I

Source: UCSD 16, 19, 8–11.

1. Again, a reflection on the Maritain phrase Oppen used as an epigraph to *The Materials:* "We awake in the same moment to ourselves and to things" (*NCP* 38).

2. From Whitehead's *Process and Reality:* "It is presupposed that no entity can be conceived in complete abstraction from the system of the universe, and that it is the business of speculative philosophy to exhibit this truth. This character is its coherence." See Alfred North Whitehead, *Process and Reality,* ed. David Ray Griffin and Donald W. Sherburne (New York: Free Press, 1978), 3.

3. The opening line of the first of Rainer Maria Rilke's *Duino Elegies,* "Who, if I cried out, would hear me among the angels' hierarchies?" ("Wer, wenn ich schriee, hörte mich denn aus der Engel / Ordnungen"). *Ahead of All Parting: The Selected Poetry and Prose of Rainer Maria Rilke,* ed. and trans. Stephen Mitchell (New York: Modern Library, 1995), 330.

4. William Bronk.

5. Diane Wakoski (1937–), poet, and correspondent of Oppen's.

6. The "you" here may be Rachel Blau DuPlessis, with whom Oppen was corresponding frequently at this time. It is also possible that Oppen is thinking here of the Guggenheim audience to whom he was introducing Diane Wakoski and William Bronk (April 1966), drafts of which introduction are scattered throughout this daybook.

7. See Yves Bonnefoy, *La beauté: Hier régnant désert* (Paris: Gallimard, 1970), 153. The context is: "Notre désir pourtant étant ton corps infirme, / Notre pitié ce coeur menant à toute boue."

8. A more accurate translation for "notre pitié ce coeur" than the one Oppen provides here would be "our pity this heart." However, given Oppen's knowledge of French—which was more than elementary but less than fluent—it is also possible that he is purposefully modifying the phrase.

9. Cf. section 1 of "Of Being Numerous" (*NCP* 163; *SP* 83).

10. These comments allude to an early version of "A Narrative" (*NCP* 150–56), originally entitled "To—." In her edition of Oppen's letters, DuPlessis speculates that the excised name is Denise Levertov (*SL* 383). See also *SL* 86, where Oppen glosses the poem in a 1963 letter to June Oppen Degnan: "'To—' means, obviously in the first section, 'to a Lady Poet, to the Domestic Poet, the poet of the happy ending—. By the end of the series it has come to be a sneaky way of saying 'to the universe.' And still, therefore, against the domestic poet. Suggests it

really offers more hope, moreover; more basis for 'the good life.'" See also "The Mind's Own Place" in the present volume, which Oppen wrote out of a critical engagement with Levertov's poetry, and which concludes with a stark rewriting of one of her presumably "happy" endings.

11. The ethical dilemma herein sketched is at the core of Oppen's political and poetic sensibilities, and echoes (unintentionally) Theodor Adorno's claim that "to write poetry after Auschwitz is barbaric." See Adorno, "Cultural Criticism and Society," in *Prisms,* trans. Samuel Weber and Shierry Weber (Cambridge, MA: MIT Press, 1981), 34. Although it is highly unlikely that Oppen was familiar with Adorno's work, the similarities between their thought at times like this are striking.

12. Cf. section 1 of "Of Being Numerous."

13. Cf. section 8 of "Of Being Numerous" (*NCP* 166; *SP* 86).

14. In the first lines of "Philai Te Kou Philai," Oppen misidentifies Thomas Eakins's *The Thinker: Portrait of Louis N. Kenton* as a "portrait by Eakins / Of the Intellectual" (*NCP* 97; *SP* 33).

15. An allusion to a series of paintings entitled *Symphony in White* by expatriated American painter James Abbott McNiel Whistler (1834–1903).

16. No indication is given as to whom Oppen is writing of here. Numerous statements elsewhere in the Daybooks and Papers offer similar comments, although more generally, on the pitfalls of poetic aspirations, and it is possible that the "he" here is hypothetical rather than specific.

17. Following precedent established by the militant black press at the time, Oppen abandoned use of the term *Negro* in the early 1960s, in favor of the term *Black,* suggesting the date of this page's composition is before 1965.

18. An important, and often neglected, aspect of Oppen's thought is his wry and often sardonic sense of humor, evident in his use of the term *bitch* here, which may be ironic.

19. Oppen may have participated—briefly and hesitantly—in an informal writing workshop in early 1966, although it is unclear who the other participants were. Notes written in the margins of his introduction to Wakoski's and Bronk's reading at the Guggenheim in April of that year reflect similarly on his experience of such groups, to which, as is clear, he reacted quite negatively.

20. It is unclear to whom Oppen refers here.

21. Cf. section 6 of "Of Being Numerous" (*NCP* 165–66; *SP* 86).

22. In a letter to June Oppen Degnan, dated September 26, 1963, Oppen meditates on Jung over three single-spaced pages, writing frankly of his preference for Jung over Freud. See *SL* 91–93, esp. 92. Unpublished letters and notes testify also to the preference.

23. From the last paragraph of Kierkegaard's "The Present Moment," no. 6, 5, subtitled "What Says the Fire Marshall?" translated here by L. M. Hollander:

> When finally the right man arrives, he who in the highest sense is called to the task for all we know, chosen early and slowly educated for this business which is, to throw light on the matter, to set fire to this jungle which is a refuge for all kinds of foolish talk and delusions and rascally tricks when he comes he will always find a nice company of addle-pated fools and twaddlers who, surely enough, do think that, perhaps, things are wrong and that "something must be done about it"; or who have taken the position, and talk a good deal about it, that it is preposterous to be self-important and talk about it. Now if he, the right man, is deceived but a single instant and thinks that it is this company who are to aid him, then it is clear he is not the right man. If he is deceived and has dealings with that company, then providence will at once take its hand off him, as not fit. But the right man will see at a glance, as the fire-marshal does, that the crowd who in the kindness of their hearts mean to help in extinguishing a conflagration by buckets and hand-squirts the right man will see that the same crowd who here, when there is a question, not of extinguishing a fire, but rather of setting something on fire, will in the kindness of their hearts wish to help with a sulphur match *sans* fire or a wet spill he will see that this crowd must be got rid of, that he must not have the least thing in common with this crowd, that he will be obliged to use the coarsest possible language against them he who perhaps at other times is anything but coarse. But the thing of supreme importance is to be rid of the crowd; for the effect of the crowd is to hamstring the whole cause by robbing it of its seriousness while heart-felt sympathy is pretended. Of course the crowd will then rage against him, against his incredible arrogance and so forth. This ought not to count with him, whether for or against, In all truly serious business the law of *either / or* prevails.

D. Anthony Storm's Commentary on Kierkegaard Web site, http://sorenkierkegaard.org/texts/text23c.htm (accessed May 29, 2007). For a more recent translation, see Søren Kierkegaard, *The Moment and Late Writings,* ed. and trans. Howard V. Hong and Edna H. Hong (Princeton, NJ: Princeton University Press, 1998), 220.

24. Diane Wakoski.

25. Oppen's edition: Søren Kierkegaard, *Purity of Heart Is to Will One Thing,* trans. Douglas V. Steere (New York: Harper and Brothers, 1948).

26. Oppen is commenting on the first section of "A Narrative" (*NCP* 150; *SP* 72).

27. In a May 1963 letter to June Oppen Degnan (*SL* 84–86), Oppen explicates an earlier version of "A Narrative" (see note 10 above). The addressee here, insofar as there is one, is most likely DuPlessis, although it bears pointing out that among Oppen's idiosyncrasies in these papers is a tendency to blur the distinction between letters to others and notes to/for himself. This may be one such instance.

28. It is unclear to whom Oppen refers here.

29. Kierkegaard, *Purity of Heart Is to Will One Thing,* 41–42:

> But repentance and remorse know how to make use of time in fear and trembling. When remorse awakens concern, whether it be in the youth, or in the old man, it awakens it always at the eleventh hour. It does not have much time at its disposal, for it is at the eleventh hour. It is not deceived by a false notion of a long life, for it

is at the eleventh hour. And in the eleventh hour one understands life in a wholly different way than in the days of youth or in the busy time of manhood or in the final moment of old age. He who repents at any other hour of the day repents in the temporal sense. He fortifies himself by a false and hasty conception of the insignificance of his guilt. He braces himself with a false and hasty notion of life's length. His remorse is not in true inwardness of spirit. Oh, eleventh hour, wherever thou art present, how all is changed! How still everything is, as if it were the midnight hour; how sober, as if it were the hour of death; how lonely, as if it were among the tombs; how solemn, as if it were within eternity. Oh, heavy hour of labor (although labor is at rest), when the account is rendered, yet there is no accuser there; when all is called by its own name, yet there is nothing said; when each improper word must be repeated, in the light of eternity! Oh, costly bargain, where remorse must pay so dearly for what seemed in the eyes of lightheartedness and busyness and proud struggling and impatient passion and the judgment of the world to be reckoned as nothing! Oh, eleventh hour, how terrible if Thou shouldst remain, how much more terrible than if death should continue through a whole life!

30. From Blaise Pascal, "Thoughts on Mind and Style," section 1 of *Pensées,* trans. W. F. Trotter, Christian Classics Ethereal Library, www.ccel.org/ccel/pascal/pensees.ii.html (accessed May 29, 2007):

The reason, therefore, that some intuitive minds are not mathematical is that they cannot at all turn their attention to the principles of mathematics. But the reason that mathematicians are not intuitive is that they do not see what is before them, and that, accustomed to the exact and plain principles of mathematics, and not reasoning till they have well inspected and arranged their principles, they are lost in matters of intuition where the principles do not allow of such arrangement. They are scarcely seen; they are felt rather than seen; there is the greatest difficulty in making them felt by those who do not of themselves perceive them. These principles are so fine and so numerous that a very delicate and very clear sense is needed to perceive them, and to judge rightly and justly when they are perceived, without for the most part being able to demonstrate them in order as in mathematics, because the principles are not known to us in the same way, and because it would be an endless matter to undertake it. We must see the matter at once, at one glance, and not by a process of reasoning, at least to a certain degree. And thus it is rare that mathematicians are intuitive and that men of intuition are mathematicians, because mathematicians wish to treat matters of intuition mathematically and make themselves ridiculous, wishing to begin with definitions and then with axioms, which is not the way to proceed in this kind of reasoning. Not that the mind does not do so, but it does it tacitly, naturally, and without technical rules; for the expression of it is beyond all men, and only a few can feel it.

DAYBOOK IV:II

Source: UCSD 19, 16, 8–11.

1. Compare to the opening of "Of Being Numerous," where Oppen alludes to (and recasts) the biblical Fall:

There are things
We live among "and to see them
Is to know ourselves."

Occurrence, a part
Of an infinite series,

The sad marvels;

Of this was told
A tale of our wickedness.
It is not our wickedness. (*NCP* 163; *SP* 83)

2. Compare to the concluding statement in "The Mind's Own Place": "But what we must have *now* . . ." (see p. 37 of present volume).

3. Diane Wakoski.

4. Robert S. Brumbaugh (1918–), philosopher, author of books on Plato and Whitehead (among others), and editor of numerous anthologies of Western philosophical texts.

5. David Antin.

6. Oppen misquotes (purposefully or otherwise) an epigraph from Charles Reznikoff's *Jerusalem the Golden* (New York: Objectivist Press, 1934). See Charles Reznikoff, *By the Waters of Manhattan* (New York: New Directions, 1962), 30. See also DuPlessis's note (*SL* 392).

7. Oppen is commenting here on the last stanza of "The Occurrences" (*NCP* 144).

8. The note is a draft of one sent to Rachel Blau DuPlessis upon her completion of graduate studies. I've included it here, as it does not appear in *SL*.

9. Oppen is commenting here on the untitled poem with which his book *Discrete Series* opens (*NCP* 5; *SP* 3).

10. According to Rachel Blau DuPlessis, Oppen might be referring to Peter Young, then married to Twyla Tharp; both were friends of the Oppens. "Dave" is David Antin.

11. Oppen misquotes the last two lines of section 2 of his poem "Image of the Engine" (*NCP* 41; *SP* 9): "In the garden! / Outside, and so beautiful."

12. Giotto di Bondone (1267–1337) was the most important Italian painter of the fourteenth century.

13. Refers to book 4 of Virgil's *Aeneid,* where Queen Dido of Carthage kills herself when she is abandoned by her lover, Aeneas. Source of full quotation is unknown, but the phrase "killed herself for love" is in canto 5, line 61, of Dante's *Inferno*.

14. William Bronk. All cited poems are found in *The World, the Worldless* (New York: New Directions, 1964).

15. Diane Wakoski.

DAYBOOK V

Source: UCSD 16, 19, 13.

1. Michael Davidson, *Ghostlier Demarcations: Modern Poetry and the Material Word* (Berkeley and Los Angeles: University of California Press, 1997), 78. Davidson's description of Oppen's practice of cutting and pasting text is much more in-depth than the one I provide here.

2. The first eight pages of the present text consist of a single "note-stack" or "palimtext." The first "page" here—marked by the symbol "+++"—records the topmost leaves of the stack, with each successive "page" revealing text that was pasted and/or taped over by Oppen. As "OBJECT in the poem" appears on the base page, it appears here more than once. (See the textual apparatus note in the front matter of this book.)

3. Text is missing in original.

4. The Black Mountain School consisted of the poets and artists affiliated with Black Mountain College in North Carolina, where poet Charles Olson was the final rector. Oppen speaks more directly of Olson's essay "Human Universe" below.

5. Jung records a number of his earliest memories, one of which Oppen's brief summary here vaguely resembles, in the opening pages of his autobiographical *Memories, Dreams, Reflections*. Jung also recounts there his "first dream," which is, indeed, a terrifying one, involving the apparition of what he calls "the subterranean God" in the visage of a man-eating "phallus." "The preacher's son" refers to Jung's self-analysis as essentially consisting of two parts: the preacher's son (Jung's father was a preacher) and the analytical psychologist/philosopher. See C. G. Jung, *Memories, Dreams, Reflections* (New York: Pantheon Books, 1963), 3–15. See also *SL* 91–93, a letter to June Oppen Degnan, in which Oppen contrasts Jung with Aquinas. That the letter dates from 1963—and that there are a number of drafts of the letter in Oppen's Daybooks (dating from roughly the same time)—suggest that Oppen's thoughts on Jung here were written years before he pasted them into the present text.

6. The source of this quote is unknown (perhaps a phrase overheard by or spoken to Oppen?). I have retained Oppen's anomalous capitalization.

7. Oppen's text breaks off here after "c——": i.e., it is not the result of a paste-over.

8. Likely an autobiographical reference to Oppen's time spent serving in World War II.

9. Oppen's rendering of Empedocles' fragment 117. See *The Fragments of Empedocles,* trans. William E. Leonard (1908; reprint, La Salle, IL: Open Court Press, 1973), 56.

10. A reference to William Wordsworth, "Ode: Intimations of Immortality from

Recollections of Early Childhood." See *The Poetical Works of Wordsworth*, ed. Paul D. Sheats (Boston: Houghton Mifflin, 1982), 353–56.

11. Section 24 of "Of Being Numerous": In this nation / Which is in some sense / Our home. Covenant! // The covenant is / There shall be peoples" (*NCP* 176; *SP* 97).

12. Poet Gary Snyder (1930–). The phrase is from an unknown source.

13. *Last Letters from Stalingrad*, trans. Franz Schneider and Charles Gullans (Westport, CT: Greenwood Press, 1961), 66. Originally published in Germany in 1954, *Last Letters* contains fragments of letters written by German soldiers trapped in Stalingrad (and eventually killed) in February 1943. The letters were originally impounded under orders from Hitler, the names of addressees and authors were excised, and they were used by Nazi brass to gauge troop morale.

14. Oppen quotes from "The Discourse of the Soul and the Body," by Melito of Sardis, an early Christian bishop and writer (died ca. A.D. 180): "What new mystery, then, is this? The Judge is judged, and holds his peace; the Invisible One is seen, and is not ashamed; the Incomprehensible is laid hold open, and is not indignant; the Illimitable is circumscribed, and doth not resist; the Impossible suffreth, and doth not avenge; the Immortal dieth, and answereth not a word; the Celestial is laid in the grave, and endureth! What new mystery is this?" Melito of Sardis, *On Pascha and Fragments*, trans. and ed. Stuart George Hall (Oxford: Oxford University Press, 1979), 80.

15. Mary Oppen; the phrase is likely hers. "Wyeth" is Andrew Wyeth (1917–), American realist painter.

16. David Antin, on whose early writing Oppen comments frequently in the late 1960s. Oppen's review of Antin's first book, *Definitions*, appears in the present volume.

17. See *NCP* 218; *SP* 127. Oppen's older sister Elizabeth (Libby) Frances Hughes died on January 25, 1960, at the age of fifty-four. Both Oppen and Libby's daughter, Diane (Andy) Meyer, believed the death to be a suicide, in keeping with coroner's reports. Oppen's half-sister, June Oppen Degnan, believed otherwise. See *SL* 184–185, 207, and especially Rachel Blau DuPlessis's note on the matter (*SL* 402).

18. The reference is to Charles Olson's 1951 essay "Human Universe." See Olson, *Collected Prose*, ed. Donald Allen and Benjamin Friedlander (Berkeley and Los Angeles: University of California Press, 1997), 155–66.

19. *Methe:* this typographical anomaly is in the original.

20. Cf. Oppen's poem "Of Hours" (*NCP* 217–19; *CP* 126–28).

21. Text missing in original.

22. Again, "Of Hours" (*NCP* 217; *CP* 126). Oppen borrows the image here partly from Simone Weil. Michael Davidson's notes to the poem (*NCP* 394–95) are especially illuminating in this regard: "Weil refers to affliction as a 'nail whose point

is applied at the very center of the soul, whose head is all necessity spreading throughout space and time." Simone Weil, *Waiting for God,* trans. Emma Craufurd (New York: Putnam, 1951), 34–35.

23. "Party on Shipboard" is the title of a poem in *Discrete Series* (*NCP* 15).

24. Francis Ponge (1899–1988), French poet and writer. The phrase is from an unknown source.

TWENTY-SIX FRAGMENTS

Source: UCSD 16, 19, 17–18.

1. A misquote—possibly an adaptation—from William Bronk's poem "Virgin and Child with Music and Numbers," in *The World, the Worldless* (New York: New Directions, 1964), 19. Bronk's line reads: "Still, the singing was and is."

2. Cf. the sestet of Keats's sonnet "On Looking into Chapman's Homer":

> Then felt I like some watcher in the skies
> When a new planet swims into his ken;
> Or like stout Cortez when with eagle eyes
> He star'd at the Pacific—and all his men
> Look'd at each other with a wild surmise—
> Silent, upon a peak in Darien.

The Complete Poems of Keats and Shelley (New York: Modern Library, 1978), 32. Keats mistakenly named Cortez in that poem, whereas the discoverer of the Pacific was actually Balboa.

3. Again, either a misquote or an adaptation of a phrase in line 4 of Gerard Manley Hopkins's sonnet "Andromeda." Gerard Manley Hopkins, *Poems* (London: Humphrey Milford, 1918), cited at Bartleby.com, www.bartleby.com/122/25. Hopkins's poem begins: "NOW Time's Andromeda on this rock rude, / With not her either beauty's equal or / Her injury's, looks off by both horns of shore, / Her flower, her piece of being, doomed dragon's food."

Index

DESIGNER: SANDY DROOKER

TEXT: 9.5/14.5 NEW CENTURY SCHOOLBOOK

DISPLAY: NEW CENTURY SCHOOLBOOK, DIN-MEDIUM

COMPOSITOR: INTEGRATED COMPOSITION SYSTEMS

INDEXER: ANDREW JORON

PRINTER AND BINDER: FRIESENS CORPORATION